MURIEL'S

MURIEL'S WEDDING

Story by
P.J. Hogan and Jocelyn Moorhouse

Screenplay by
P.J. Hogan

FOURTH ESTATE · *LONDON*

First published in Great Britain in 1995 by
Fourth Estate Limited
6 Salem Road
London W2 4BU

Copyright © 1994 by P.J. Hogan

A catalogue record for this book is available
from the British Library.

ISBN 1-85702-367-6

Typeset by SX Composing Ltd, Rayleigh, Essex
Printed in Great Britain by Cox and Wyman Ltd,
Reading, Berkshire

Muriel's Wedding was written in desperation. For over eight years I struggled to get my first feature film made and I'd come close a number of times. I directed a telemovie in the mid-eighties which I'd hoped would lead to more films. It didn't. I was removed from the production and it was recut and remixed. It turned up four years later on television in non-ratings period. Then there was the script that made it as far as pre-production. The crew was hired and I was in the middle of casting, when suddenly the money wasn't there any more. Our mysterious Greek shipping tycoons never did sign the appropriate contracts and probably never planned to. This left me with an empty bank account (Do first-time directors every get paid?), a lot of disappointed actors and the feeling that perhaps I should be thinking about a career change. A change to what I didn't know. I decided to take one last shot at it and write about something I by now knew intimately: failure.

I'd sit in a coffee shop that made great cheap cappuccino and report into a notebook the details of my life of poverty. I hoped that one day a story or a character would emerge from these random jottings, somehow giving it all meaning. Across the road from the coffee shop was a bridalwear store called – I swear – Cinderellas. I would watch the young girls enter the store looking non-descript in their everyday clothes and then see them appear in the front window transformed into brides. Every hour I watched somebody's dream come true. I was aware that though Cinderellas looked open to all young girls, it wasn't. It was a club meant for the engaged only. I started to plot a way for one of the unchosen to invade the world of the privileged few. Why shouldn't every woman have the opportunity to live out the fantasy that she has been tempted with since childhood? Why should she be denied the princess experience just because the prince was late in coming? The idea was born of a girl who invades this world going from store to store in a city trying on bridal gowns, inventing fictitious fiancés who want her, and all the while remaining single. I called this serial bride Muriel.

I worked on the script for about eight months and when I thought it was ready we looked for the money to make it. There followed three years of rejection. The money people disliked Muriel for all the reasons I loved her: she was gauche, awkward, overweight, neither intellectual nor creative and obsessed with getting married. They suggested I set aside the idea or perhaps tell it another way with a re-vamped central character – thinner, more attractive perhaps. Eventually, Muriel found a home with CIBY 2000, a French company who loved her for herself.

Directing is another set of obstacles to overcome, but what I have learned as a writer is simply never to give up. Nobody understands your idea better than you and most times the stuff that nobody likes is what is best about it. An original screenplay is uncharted territory and you have to be willing to sail directly into the reefs and the storms with no guarantee that you will return with anything but the experience.

P. J. Hogan

MURIEL'S WEDDING

Cast:

MURIEL	Toni Collette
BILL	Bill Hunter
RHONDA	Rachel Griffiths
BETTY	Jeanie Drynan
DEIDRE	Gennie Nevinson
BRICE	Matt Day
DAVID VAN ARCKLE	Daniel Lapaine
TANIA	Sophie Lee
JANINE	Belinda Jarrett
CHERYL	Rosalind Hammond
NICOLE	Pippa Grandison
KEN BLUNDELL	Chris Haywood
PERRY	Daniel Wyllie
JOAN	Gabby Millgate
PENELOPE	Katie Saunders
MALCOLM	Dene Kermond
GIRL AT WEDDING	Susan Prior
CHOOK	Nathan Kaye
TANIA'S MOTHER	Cecily Polson
LEO HIGGINS	Rob Steele
STORE DETECTIVE	Genevieve Picot
CONSTABLE SAUNDERS	Richard Sutherland
CONSTABLE GILLESPIE	Steve Smith
CHINESE WAITRESS	Jeamin Lee
CHINESE MAITRE D'	Jon-Claire Lee
AKIRA	Kuni Hashimoto
VICTOR KEINOSUKE	Ken Senga
ISLAND M.C.	Des Rodgers
RESTAURANT BOYS	Rohan Jones
	Scott Hall-Watson
	Craig Olson
	Justin Witham

SC. I   TITLE CARD

A title card reads: THE BOUQUET

SC. 2   EXT. YARD OF BEACH HOUSE – DAY

A bouquet of pink and white flowers materialises out of a blue sky and hurtles downwards towards a group of young girls, all reaching upwards.

Muriel Heslop stands in the centre of the group. She is a plain, plump girl in her early twenties. She wears a tightly fitting strapless leopard-skin print dress. An Instamatic camera hangs from a strap around her neck.

The bouquet lands in her hands.

Guests, standing before a nearby house, applaud. The carport beneath the house is decorated for a wedding reception.

Clapping loudly is a young man dressed as a groom. His name is Chook. He has shoulder-length blond hair and holds a can of beer. His ruffled shirt is open to his stomach.

The excited bride, Tania, turns.

                    TANIA
Who caught it?

Muriel stands blinking at her catch. Two girls, dressed as bridesmaids, stand beside her. They are Janine and Cheryl. Both are painfully thin and have matching crimped hair.

                    CHERYL
                    (*bitterly*)
Muriel.

                    TANIA
Cheryl! I told you to stand near the buffet table.

                    CHERYL
I was standing near the buffet table. It didn't come anywhere near me. It went straight to Muriel.

Muriel grins.

I

MURIEL

Looks like I'm next.

Muriel pulls a face – something she does when she's feeling self-conscious. Cheryl bursts into tears.

TANIA

Cheryl . . . I can throw it, again.

CHERYL

You can't do that. It went to her.

TANIA

Muriel, throw it again.

Muriel looks reluctant.

JANINE

What's the use of you having it, Muriel? No one's ever gonna marry you. You've never even had a boyfriend. Cheryl's been going with Shane for over six weeks. She's next.

TANIA

Muriel, don't be selfish.

Muriel contemplates her bouquet and then throws it to Cheryl. Cheryl looks at the bouquet and bursts into tears again. She hurls it at Muriel.

CHERYL

Keep your stupid bouquet! Shane and I broke up last night!

Cheryl runs off. Tania follows her.

TANIA

Cheryl . . .

JANINE
(*angrily, to Muriel*)

Now look what you've done. You didn't even buy a new dress.

MURIEL

Yes, I did . . .

Janine joins Tania and Cheryl. Muriel picks up her bouquet.

SC. 3   INT. LOUNGEROOM OF HOUSE

In the loungeroom of the house two women cut up what's left of the three-tiered wedding cake. Muriel takes a paper bag containing a piece of cake and walks towards the loungeroom stairs. She passes a small group of middle-aged men.

HIGGINS

G'day, Muriel. That's an eye-catchin' dress? How's your Dad?
(*not waiting for an answer*)
Give him my card. Tell him Leo Higgins reckons he's a great man
– the best Council President this town's ever had.

A pinch-faced woman, standing near Muriel, turns during this conversation and looks with surprise at Muriel's dress. Muriel leaves Higgins and walks down the stairs. The pinch-faced woman watches her go and moves to a telephone. She dials a number and begins to talk surreptitiously.

SC. 4   INT. BENEATH HOUSE

Muriel enters the hall that leads on to the reception area. A noise stops her. It is a soft moan, and it came from the laundry room which is not visible from the stairs.

Muriel moves to the laundry room. The moaning continues.

Through a crack in the laundry door she can see Chook the groom and chief bridesmaid Nicole locked in a passionate kiss. Nicole sits on the washing machine, her arms wrapped around Chook's back. Chook's hands emerge from beneath Nicole's skirt with the thick roll of her underpants and stockings. Nicole yanks down his trousers and underpants.

Muriel watches wide-eyed, as the two begin to fuck.

NICOLE

Oh, Chook . . . Chook . . . Chook . . .

Chook, without looking back, kicks closed the laundry door. Muriel

*listens as the washing machine is switched on and the hum of the first cycle
muffles their grunting.*

SC. 5   EXT. YARD OF HOUSE

*Outside the house, a police car comes up the drive. Tania, Janine, Cheryl
and other guests watch as two young constables climb out of the car. The
pinch-faced woman approaches them and shows her identification.*

SC. 6   INT. RECEPTION AREA

*Muriel, sipping some punch, stands alone in the reception area. The other
guests become quiet as the two constables and the pinch-faced woman
(who is a store detective) walk through the reception area and stop before
Muriel.*

> STORE DETECTIVE
> (*indicating Muriel*)

That's her.

> FIRST CONSTABLE

Miss, we'd like to have a word with you about your dress.

> MURIEL
> (*terrified*)

What's wrong with it?

> STORE DETECTIVE

You stole it. I saw you.

SC. 7   EXT. YARD OF HOUSE

*The constables lead Muriel to the police car. The store detective walks
beside the First Constable.*

> FIRST CONSTABLE

Give me your work number and if she can't turn up the receipt,
I'll call you for a statement.

STORE DETECTIVE

Ask for Dianne. Senior store detective.
> (*smiles*)

I'm so pleased. I had a perfect arrest record until I lost her in Boyswear.

FIRST CONSTABLE

How'd you know she'd be here?

STORE DETECTIVE

I didn't. I'm the groom's cousin.
> (*shrugs*)

It's just one of those happy little coincidences.

The Second Constable places Muriel in the police car.

Beneath the house, Nicole and Chook – looking slightly mussed – enter the reception area.

NICOLE
> (*to a nearby girl*)

What's going on.

GIRL

They're arresting Muriel for wearing an ugly dress.

NICOLE

Oh, no. Tania's wedding day's ruined.

Tania's mother runs up to the police car.

TANIA'S MOTHER

Here Muriel, you forgot your wedding cake.

She hands Muriel her paper packet.

TANIA'S MOTHER

If you put it under your pillow you'll dream of your future husband.

MURIEL
> (*grateful*)

Thanks for inviting me.

6

Muriel looks at Tania, Cheryl and Janine.

MURIEL

I told you it was a new dress.

The police car drives off. Muriel looks humiliated as some small boys throw confetti over the car.

SC. 8   EXT. OUTSKIRTS OF TOWN

The police car roars past a large sign which reads: Welcome to Porpoise Spit, a Paradise of Sun, Surf and Shopping. There is a drawing of a wet porpoise dancing beside a mall.

SC. 9   INT. HESLOP BEDROOM

Bill Heslop, a ruddy-faced stout man in his early fifties, is on the telephone. Wearing shorts and a singlet, he sits at a wooden roll-top desk which overflows with papers. Beside Bill is a smeary picture window which affords a view of the distant ocean.

BILL

It's as good as approved. No, it's not. But it will be. The Porpoise Spit Council backs me up 100 per cent. Look, we'll talk about it over dinner tonight. Yeah, I'll bring the whole family.

Outside the bedroom door a twelve-year-old girl in leotards executes clumsy ballet steps. This is Penelope.

BILL

Penelope, do that somewhere else!
                    (*calls after her*)
Ask Mum to make me a cup o' tea.

SC. 10   INT. LOUNGEROOM/KITCHEN

Penelope runs into the loungeroom, passing the walk-in kitchen. Standing in the kitchen, lost in a daydream, is Betty Heslop. Betty, in her late forties, is small and wide. She has short curly hair and a gentle expression

7

PENELOPE

Mum, make Dad a cup of tea.

BETTY
(*snaps out of her daydream*)

Oh. What? Tea. Yes.

Betty moves about the kitchen, still a little dazed, not sure where the cups are.

Penelope sits into a chair in the spacious and messy loungeroom. The television shows a cricket match. Watching are Perry (aged 20), Malcolm (aged 15) and Joan (aged 18). All are overweight, with Joan being the largest. She wears a white t-shirt upon which is printed the smiling face of Bill Heslop. A slogan above Bill's face reads: 'Vote 1 Bill Heslop. You Can't Stop Progress'. Joan's breasts distort Bill's face, expanding his forehead.

On television a ball is caught and Malcolm and Perry cheer. Perry is six foot tall, dishevelled and unshaven. When he speaks he is often incoherent. Malcolm is sullen.

JOAN
(*referring to television*)

That was a good one, Perry, wasn't it? Hey?

Perry ignores her.

JOAN
(*loudly, but to herself*)

Alright, don't answer me then.

In the kitchen, Betty is filling a cup with water from the sink tap. She drops a tea-bag into the cup and places it inside a microwave oven. She presses a few buttons and the cup slowly turns under the microwave light.

Joan looks out the verandah doors to see the police car arrive. Muriel gets out of the car and looks up at the house.

JOAN

Muriel's back.

SC. II INT. HESLOP LOUNGEROOM

Bill, who has pulled on a shirt, stands before the two constables and Muriel. Betty, looking nervous, stands nearby. Perry and Malcolm are on the back landing of the house peering in through a window.

BILL

Muriel, did you steal this dress?

MURIEL

No.

BILL

Where'd you get the money to buy it? You 'aven't had a job in two years.

Muriel, aware of the constables' gaze, looks embarrassed.

MURIEL

Mum gave it to me.

BILL
(*to Betty*)

This true?

BETTY

Er . . . No . . . er . . . oh . . . I don't think so.

BILL
(*to Muriel*)

Find the receipt. Go on.

Muriel walks down the hall towards her bedroom.

BILL
(*to First Constable*)

What happens if she can't find it.

FIRST CONSTABLE

We'll have to contact the store and see if they want to press charges.

BILL

You know who I am?

FIRST CONSTABLE
(*nods, intimidated*)
Yes, sir, Councillor Heslop.

BILL
Who are you?

FIRST CONSTABLE
I'm Constable Saunders, this is Constable Gillespie.

BILL
Saunders? You're not Graham Saunders' oldest, are you?

FIRST CONSTABLE
(*nods*)
Brad.

Muriel watches from behind her bedroom door. Joan hides in an adjacent doorway.

JOAN
(*whispers to Muriel*)
You're terrible, Muriel.

BILL
(*turning on the charm*)
Young Brad. I haven't seen you since you played fullback for the Porpoise Spit Giants. How's your Dad? How's he recovering from that stroke?

FIRST CONSTABLE
Better than he was.

BILL
He's a great man, your Dad. You tell him I said that. Tell him Councillor Bill Heslop says he's a great man. How 'bout a beer? A cold one before you get back to work.

Bill turns quickly to Betty.

BILL
Betty.

Betty jumps, startled.

BETTY

Yes. What?

BILL

Get the young fellas a beer.

BETTY

Oh, yes . . .

Betty moves to the kitchen.

BILL

Take a seat, boys.

Bill sits on the couch beside the First Constable.

BILL

Your Dad's a great mate. Is there anything I can do for him?

SC. 12   INT. MURIEL'S BEDROOM

Muriel leafs through a bridal wear magazine. She hears voices and moves to her window. The two constables walk back to their car. They wave to Bill, who stands on the verandah, and drive off with a friendly toot of the horn.

Muriel switches on her tape-recorder and Abba's 'Dancing Queen' begins to play. She sits on her bed and takes her piece of wedding cake out of its packet. She contemplates eating it, but returns it to its packet and places it under her pillow. She lies back, closes her eyes and waits . . .

SC. 13   INT. BILL'S CAR – NIGHT

Through the rear vision mirror Bill's eyes glare at Muriel.

Muriel sits in the back seat of the car, squashed between Joan and Malcolm. She is aware of Bill's gaze and shifts nervously in her seat. The family rides in silence, no one daring to look at Muriel.

Inside a Chinese restaurant, located in a Leagues Club, Bill and his family sit at a window table. Behind them, on a lower level, are rows of poker machines. Seated beside Bill are two Japanese businessmen. One is an urbane-looking man by the name of Victor Keinosuke. Muriel sits beside Victor. A waiter places a tray of honeyed prawns on the table.

BILL

Look at this.
                    (*to waiter*)
You're a beautiful man, Charlie Chan. Beautiful. How's your uncle?
                    (*to Victor*)
I got his uncle out of China, you know. Talked to the blokes in Immigration – Ian Mackay and the boys – and they got Charlie Chan's uncle out of China.

WAITER
(*referring to Bill*)

This is a great man.

BILL

Charlie, this is Victor Keinosuke and his mate Akira. They're out from China – Japan. They're good mates and I want you to take good care of 'em. They're building a resort at Wallum Beach, and they might need a Chinese restaurant in it. So keep that food coming.

The waiter moves off.

BILL
(*to Victor*)

It's all on the house, because I got his uncle out of China.

*AKIRA

You've done a lot for the people of this town, Bill.

BILL
(*pleased*)

Who told you that?

*Amendment (28/10/93)

13

*AKIRA

You did.

BILL

I like helping out. I ran for state Government once.
(looks at Joan Jnr)
Joan, stand up, show 'em your shirt.

Joan, still wearing the campaign shirt with Bill's face on it, grins and stands.

BILL

'Bill Heslop. You Can't Stop Progress.'

JOAN

He lost.

Bill glares at Betty. Betty looks uncomfortable.

*Amendment (28/10/93)

BILL

Yeah . . . Missed out on the postal votes. But it left me with a lot of friends. Did I show you this picture of me an' Bob Hawke?

(*to Joan*)

You can sit down now, Joan.

Bill takes a faded newspaper clipping from his pocket and hands it to Victor and Akira. It shows Bill shaking Bob Hawke's hand.

BILL

Taken durin' the campaign. In a way I'm glad I didn't get in. I can do more for this place on a grass roots level. Highrises, malls, resorts. The Porpoise Spit Council believes in progress. Muriel, when Victor was nineteen he was a millionaire.

(*to Victor*)

Muriel's on the dole. So's Perry.

MURIEL

I've got a job interview next week. An apprentice locksmith.

BETTY

Oh. That sounds wonderful. Doesn't it, Bill?

BILL

(*oozing contempt*)

You're a bit old to be an apprentice, aren't you?

Muriel looks embarrassed.

BILL

You're a bit old for everything.

(*to Victor*)

After she failed high school, I get her into this secretarial course run by a friend of mine. Cost me three hundred dollars a term for two years, and she comes out and she can't even type. Two years, two thousand dollars and she can't even type.

MURIEL

I could type.

15

BILL

I get her a job with my solicitors and after one month they ring me up and Stevey Mason says to me 'Bill, we have to let her go, she can't type.'

MURIEL

If I couldn't type, why did they give me my secretarial diploma?

BILL

Because I paid for it. Now she sits at home like a dead weight, watching TV, sleeping all day and getting arrested at weddings. You're useless.

Bill looks around the table at his children.

BILL

You're all useless. A useless bunch of no-hopers.

Bill looks towards the entrance of the restaurant and his face lights up.

BILL
(*exclaims loudly*)

There's Deidre Chambers!

Deidre Chambers, a dark-haired thin woman in her early forties, stands in the entrance of the restaurant. She wears a high-collared, neatly fitting dress that does not hide her ripe sensuality.

BILL

What a coincidence!
(*waving and calling*)

Deidre! Deidre!

Deidre feigns surprise.

DEIDRE

Bill!
(*approaching the table*)

What a coincidence.

BILL

Pull up a chair. Penelope, shift over.

(gesturing towards the Japanese)

Deidre, Victor Keinosuke and his mate Akira. They're all the way from China – Japan.

(to Victor)

Deidre's a sales representative for Radiant Cosmetics.

DEIDRE

(correcting tone)

Beauty Consultant, Bill.

BILL

(happily)

Sorry, Beauty Consultant.

DEIDRE

(to Victor)

Sales representative sounds so common. I advise women on the right lipstick, base, eyeliner . . . of course you'd know all about make-up, your wives are probably geishas.

BETTY

You're looking lovely, Deidre.

DEIDRE

Muriel, how was that wedding?

MALCOLM

She was arrested.

DEIDRE

That's lovely. Don't you wish you were twenty-two again, Betty? Remember that age?

BETTY

Oh, yes. What?

DEIDRE

I bet you were a terror at twenty-two. Bill, was she a terror?

Bill gives a non-committal grunt.

MALCOLM

Mum never did anything, did you, Mum?

BETTY

That's right. Nothing at all. I lived in Canberra and . . . oh, there was nothing open. Not like now, where everything's open, all the shops. Sometimes we'd go dancing. Remember that, Bill? At the Starlight room, we'd go . . .

BILL
(interrupting, looking about)

Where's Charlie Chan with that food?

BETTY
(immediately looking about)

Oh, yes. Where is he?

Muriel looks at her mother sadly.

SC. 15   INT. LEAGUES CLUB — NIGHT

Penelope and Malcolm play on pinball machines in the children's games room, while Betty, Joan and Perry feed coins into poker machines.

Bill leads Victor and Akira to a large window which shows a view of Porpoise Spit, its lights glimmering in the night.

*AKIRA

A beautiful view.

BILL

Holds a lot of promise.

Deidre walks with Muriel away from the window.

DEIDRE

Your Dad was telling me you're unemployed, Muriel.

Muriel nods.

DEIDRE

Would you like to work for me?

*Amendment (28/10/93)

18

MURIEL
(*pause*)
Do you think I could be an actress?

DEIDRE
Muriel, I'm offering you a job as a sales representative.

MURIEL
What about a model?

DEIDRE
(*testy*)
Do you want the job or not?

MURIEL
Alright.

SC. 16   EXT. STREET IN PORPOISE SPIT – DAY

Muriel looks through the window of a bridal wear store. Inside a radiant young girl, outfitted as a bride, is attended by an admiring manageress and her assistant.

SC. 17   INT. CAKE SHOP – DAY

Muriel sits in a cake shop eating a chocolate éclair. She looks at the photos she took at the wedding. There is a group of Tania the bride, Janine, Cheryl and Nicole. Muriel appears on the edge of the photo.

Muriel carefully tears herself off the photo. She goes through the other photos and rips herself out.

SC. 18   INT. NIGHTCLUB – NIGHT

Muriel approaches a side booth in a nightclub. In the booth Tania is crying into a napkin. She is comforted by Janine, Cheryl and Nicole. Muriel sits with the girls.

TANIA

He couldn't do it.

(sniffs)

So I . . .

(sheepishly)

. . . you know. And I noticed there was lipstick on it.

JANINE

On what?

TANIA

His dick. He said he was having an affair.

Nicole looks worried. Muriel looks at her.

JANINE

Who with?

TANIA

Rose Biggs.

NICOLE
(stunned)

Rose Biggs?

TANIA

He said they didn't sleep together, she only sucks him off.

JANINE

Why?

TANIA

Out of respect for me.

JANINE

The bitch.

NICOLE
(*furious*)

The bastard.

TANIA
(*miserably*)

What am I going to do? I'm a bride. I'm supposed to be euphoric.

CHERYL

Come on the cruise with us. Cash in your ticket to Bali and have your honeymoon with us.

TANIA
(*after brief contemplation*)

Alright.

The girls cheer.

MURIEL

What cruise?

The girls become furtive.

CHERYL

Just around the Pacific Islands.

JANINE

We didn't think you could afford it because you don't have a job.

MURIEL
(*brightly*)

Yes, I do. I got one last night. I'm a beauty consultant.

JANINE
(*to Nicole*)

Let's tell her. We were gonna tell her after the cruise, let's tell her now.

NICOLE
(*pause. Then firmly*)

Muriel . . .

CHERYL
(*suddenly upset*)

Wait. Let her finish her 'Orgasm'.

Muriel apprehensively drains her glass.

NICOLE

Muriel . . . people think we're mad, but that's just us. We're ragers. People invite us to parties and they know we'll just have a good time.

JANINE

We're mad.

CHERYL

Party, party, party.

NICOLE

That's our image. You know what I mean?

MURIEL
(*nods*)

We're mad.

NICOLE

We don't want you hanging around us any more.

A look of fear crosses Muriel's face.

MURIEL

I didn't steal the dress. It was a mistake.

NICOLE

It's not the dress, it's you. We've told you a thousand times how to do your hair, but you never listen.

CHERYL

You never wear the right clothes.

JANINE

You're fat.

CHERYL

You like the wrong music. Nobody listens to Abba any more – we all listen to The Baby Animals and The Sugarcubes.

NICOLE

You bring us down, Muriel.

JANINE

You embarrass us.

Muriel sits quietly for a moment.

MURIEL
(*earnestly*)

I know I'm not normal, but I'm trying to change. I'm trying to become more like you, more of a . . . a human.

NICOLE

It's too late.

MURIEL

I can change.

NICOLE

You'll still be you.

Muriel looks devastated.

TANIA
(*gently*)

Muriel, you have to find friends on your own level – like I found Chook. He's up on my level. Marrying him was the happiest day of my life.

Tears begin to flow down Tania's cheeks.

TANIA

I love him so much.

The other girls comfort Tania.

TANIA

The bastard! I'll show him. I'll go on this cruise and sleep with a thousand men.

Muriel, her head bowed, is crying.

MURIEL

I'm not nothing.

JANINE
(*angrily*)

Muriel, can't you think of anyone but yourself? Tania's upset.

MURIEL
(*loud*)

I'm not nothing!

Muriel sobs loudly.

NICOLE

Muriel, you're embarrassing us again.

24

SC. 19   EXT. HESLOP BACK YARD – DAY

Perry runs around the large, untidy back yard tossing and kicking an empty milk carton like a football. He mutters an announcer's commentary on his performance in the 'match', and also provides the wild whistles and cheers of the crowd.

Bill, looking disgusted, watches Perry from the loungeroom window. After a few moments he can bear no more.

> BILL

Perry!

Perry freezes mid-play.

> BILL

Wake up to yourself!

Bill leaves the window. Perry stands quietly for a moment and then, muttering his commentary, resumes his game.

SC. 20   INT. MURIEL'S BEDROOM – DAY

Through the half-open doorway of Muriel's bedroom we see Bill move from the window to the kitchen counter. He gathers up his council papers.

> BILL
> (*tersely, to Betty*)

Muriel up?

> BETTY
> (*calls up the hallway*)

Muriel! Get up! It's nearly ten thirty.

Muriel lies awake in bed. Beside her, on her dresser, is the bouquet standing in a cup of water. Dry petals fall from the dying flowers.

> BILL

Make sure she sees Deidre Chambers about that job. Write her out a blank cheque for the cosmetics.

> BETTY

A blank cheque. How much for?

BILL
(*exasperated*)

It's a blank cheque. She fills in the amount when Deidre tells her what it is.

Bill stomps down the stairs.

BILL

Get Perry to mow that back yard, and clean this place up. It's a pigsty.

BETTY
(*angrily*)

Joan! Turn the TV off! Clean this place up! It's a pigsty!

Muriel sits up. Betty enters her bedroom.

BETTY

Muriel, you have to get up and see Deidre Chambers about that job. I have to give you a blank cheque.

Betty sits beside Muriel and opens her chequebook.

BETTY

It's wonderful of Deidre to give you work. She's a wonderful person, I don't care what anyone says.

MURIEL

What who says?

Betty writes the date on a cheque.

BETTY
(*agitated*)

Oh . . . people who've never liked Dad. Those greenies, and those terrible women at the Post Office.

MURIEL

What are they saying?

BETTY

Should I make it out to Deidre Chambers or Radiant Cosmetics?

Muriel looks at the chequebook and it registers for the first time.

MURIEL

A blank cheque?

Betty nods.

MURIEL
(*after a beat*)

Cash.
(*and then quickly*)
What do they say about Deidre and Dad?

BETTY
(*becoming emotional*)
Oh . . . well . . . they say that they go driving together at night.
He's just showing her his developments, that's all.

Muriel watches as Betty makes the cheque out to 'Cash' and signs it.

MURIEL

His what?

BETTY
Building sites. Oh. I suppose everyone thinks I'm ridiculous. I
know I let myself go. I don't know what to do.

She gives the cheque to Muriel.

MURIEL
I'm gonna be a success, Mum. I'm going to get married and
I'm gonna be a success.

BETTY
(*cheered by Muriel's mood*)
I know you are. Dad just wants to be proud of you, that's all.

MURIEL
I'll show him. I'll show them all.

BETTY
I know you will.

SC. 21   EXT. OCEAN – DAY

Abba sing 'Ring Ring' as we cut to a wideshot of the Pacific ocean. A small green island shines like an emerald in the turquoise water.

*SC. 22   EXT. POOL – DAY

Around the resort pool, holidaymakers partake in resort activities. Waiters serve drinks to people lounging beside the pool.

In the pool, wearing bikinis, are Tania and Cheryl. They sit on the broad brown shoulders of two young men. The girls wrestle, Tania almost toppling Cheryl from her beefy perch.

Beside the pool, in deckchairs, are Janine and Nicole with two more boys. They cheer the wresting match.

Tania plunges into the water. One of the young men gathers her up into his arms. Janine aims her camera at the pool.

JANINE

This one's for Chook!

Tania slips her arm around the young man's neck and smiles.

Later, and a crowd is seated before a small rostrum on the deck. A talent quest is in progress. Tania, Nicole, Janine and Cheryl, dressed as Hawaiian maidens, lip-sync and dance badly to 'The Tide is High'.

At a nearby table the boys clap and whistle.

Now the boys are on stage. Wearing Hawaiian shirts and board shorts, they mime enthusiastically to Peter Allen's 'I Go to Rio' and strum badminton racquets like guitars.

The girls, seated at the table, clap and cheer.

NICOLE
(referring to their empty glasses)

Whose shout is it?

*CHERYL

*Janine's.

*Amendment (28/10/93)

28

Janine looks towards the poolside bar and screams.

Seated a few feet away, at a table near the bar, is Muriel. She wears dark sunglasses, a big floppy hat, a white shirt over a one-piece bathing suit and zinc cream on her nose. Sipping a cocktail through a straw, she stares at the girls.

After a moment of stunned silence, the girls get up from their table. They surround Muriel, who looks elsewhere. She looks up and removes her sunglasses.

MURIEL
(*acting surprised*)

Hi.

(*suppressing a smirk*)

What a coincidence.

Tania is enraged. She can barely speak. She picks up the cocktail glass and throws the contents into Muriel's face.

TANIA

You mental case! You keep away from us!

*Amendment (28/10/93)

Tania strides off. The others follow, except for Cheryl. She is wearing a grass skirt, a coconut shell bra and plastic fruit on her head. She looks at Muriel sadly.

CHERYL

You've got no dignity, Muriel.

Cheryl walks off. Muriel wipes her face.

SC. 23   INT. SHIP RESTAURANT — NIGHT

Nicole, Janine and Cheryl sit at a table in the crowded ship restaurant. They comfort Tania, who is crying.

TANIA

She's ruined my honeymoon. I may as well be with Chook.

Muriel, wearing an expensive tight red velvet evening gown and dark sunglasses, sweeps into the restaurant. A steward seats Muriel at a nearby table. She peruses the wine list.

MURIEL
(*to steward*)

I'll have a bottle of 'Mote'.

STEWARD

'Moet'. Very good.

MURIEL

And can I send something cheap to table five?

The steward leaves. Sitting adjacent to Muriel is a short, plump young woman with wavy black hair. She also wears dark sunglasses. This is Rhonda Epinstall, aged twenty-three.

RHONDA

Are you Muriel Heslop?

MURIEL
(*instantly terrified*)

No.

RHONDA

Yes, you are.

MURIEL
(*in a panic*)

Why?

RHONDA

I don't know why, you just are.

Rhonda removes her sunglasses, revealing bright but dark-ringed eyes.

RHONDA

Rhonda Epinstall. We went to high school together. You dropped out in year ten, I dropped out in year eleven. I knew it was you.
(*to the diner who sits between herself and Muriel*)
Swap seats.

Rhonda sits in the chair beside Muriel.

RHONDA

Are you married now?

MURIEL

What?

RHONDA

You said you weren't Muriel Heslop. If you've changed your name, I thought you must've got married.

MURIEL

No. Yes.
(*pause*)
I'm engaged.

RHONDA
(*smiles*)

Anyone I know?

MURIEL

What? Who? Tim.

RHONDA

Who?

MURIEL

What?

RHONDA

Tim who?

MURIEL

Simms.

RHONDA

Tim Simms. Don't know him. What's he like?

MURIEL
(*shrugs*)

Like no one.

RHONDA
(*offering packet*)

Smoke?

MURIEL

What?

RHONDA

I shouldn't. I'm an asthmatic.
(*lights up*)
I'm living in Sydney now, and I do all the things my Mum said not
to: drink, smoke and fuck before marriage.

*Now Muriel and Rhonda walk up the side of a buffet table. Rhonda
loads her tray with desserts.*

RHONDA

So, where is he?

MURIEL

Who?

RHONDA

Tim Simms.

Muriel's mind races to make up an answer.

RHONDA

I'm on to you.

Muriel looks nervous.

RHONDA

You're not wearing an engagement ring, you're here without your fiancé . . .
(*triumphantly*)
You're out for a good time, aren't you, Muriel? A last fling.

MURIEL
(*smiles*)

I s'pose so.

RHONDA

You're wicked. Well stick with me 'cause I'm wicked too. My whole life is one last fling after another.

MURIEL
(*grins*)

Remember Tania Degano? She got married – to Chook.

RHONDA

To what?

MURIEL

Chook – Peter Vernell.

RHONDA
(*nods*)

I remember them. What a pair of arseholes. They deserve each other. Whenever I think about how revolting Porpoise Spit was I think of Tania Degano and those idiots she hung around with. They made my life hell. Do you ever dream about what you'd say to them if you saw them now?

MURIEL

I do see them now.

Rhonda looks nonplussed.

33

They're over there.

Rhonda chokes on her cigarette.

RHONDA

What are they doing here?

MURIEL

They're on Tania's honeymoon. Chook couldn't come.

Rhonda coughs violently. She places a Ventilon inhaler in her mouth and squirts it.

SC. 24   EXT. MARKET – DAY

In a crowded island market Tania, Janine, Cheryl and Nicole try on handcrafted jewellery.

RHONDA'S VOICE

Tania!

Tania and the girls turn to find Muriel and Rhonda standing behind them.

RHONDA

What a fantastic surprise!

TANIA

I don't believe it. I haven't seen you since Porpoise Spit High.

RHONDA

How are you?

TANIA
(*displays her wedding ring*)

Married.

RHONDA

Muriel told me. Turkey.

TANIA

Chook.

34

RHONDA

Chook. That's right. Congratulations.

TANIA

Come and have a drink with us.

RHONDA

(*in mock deference*)

Really?

(*feigning incredulity*)

You want to have a drink with me?

TANIA

(*taking the bait*)

We can't let you spend the entire cruise alone.

Muriel looks stung.

TANIA

We're not in school any more, Rhonda. You don't have to feel
you're not good enough for us now.

RHONDA

(*amused*)

I don't?

TANIA

We'll judge you on who you are now, not on who you were. If
I feel you've changed I'll tell you. I'm honest
(*directed to Muriel*)
– unlike some people. I tell it like it is.

RHONDA

The truth?

TANIA

(*nods*)

Yes.

RHONDA

I tell the truth too. Nicole's having an affair with Chook.
Muriel saw them fucking in the laundry on your wedding day.

Tania's mouth drops open. Muriel stares at Rhonda.

> RHONDA

Stick your drink up your arse, Tania. I'd rather swallow razor blades than drink with you.

Rhonda turns to leave.

> RHONDA

By the way, I'm not alone, I'm with Muriel.

Rhonda and Muriel link arms and walk off through the crowded market. Tania and Nicole look stunned. We hear the dramatic opening chord of Abba's 'Waterloo'.

*SC. 25   EXT. RESTAURANT – NIGHT

Muriel and Rhonda, dressed as Anna and Frida from Abba (white satin pant-suits, sequined belts, silver boots and voluminous wigs), dance on a * small rostrum lip-syncing to the song. A banner proclaims 'Star Search'.

The audience sit at tables before the rostrum. Tania, Janine and Cheryl sit up front with three boys. Tania's face is tight with rage. Camera moves left to reveal Nicole sporting a black eye.

Muriel is nervous and can barely remember the dance routine she and Rhonda have worked out, but after a few bars her confidence builds. Rhonda leads the way, her arms waving, her boots stomping.

The audience begins to cheer the performance. The boys seated beside Tania and the girls shout encouragement. Tania glares at Nicole. Nicole, her bottom lip trembling, stares ahead.

Muriel and Rhonda bounce around the stage, sequins falling from their outfits. Their movements gain fluidity and their lip-sync is near perfect.

The audience clap and cheer wildly.

Tania suddenly leaps from her seat and attacks Nicole. They fall to the deck, scratching and punching. Janine and Cheryl scream. The boys leap to their feet and cheer the fight.

*Amendment (28/10/93)

Muriel and Rhonda fly towards the climax of their song.

The song continues as we jump-cut to the end of the contest. The M.C. bounds out from the side of the stage, his face full of enthusiasm.

*M.C.
(*to audience*)
Weren't they beautiful? Weren't they fantastic girls?
(*to girls*)
I love you both.
(*back to audience*)
So . . . what do you think, audience? Do we love them or do we love them?

The M.C. grins and cups a hand over his ear. The audience leap to their feet and applaud. The large wooden needle on the clap-o-meter hits the highest score.

The M.C. stands between Muriel and Rhonda and lifts their hands into the air. An assistant presents the girls with a magnum of champagne. They leap about excitedly.

*MURIEL
(*overwhelmed*)
Thanks, Barry.

Tania – comforted by Janine and Cheryl – sobs on the table. Nicole staggers away, a serviette clamped over her bloodied nose.

*Amendment (28/10/93)

MURIEL'S VOICE (OVER)
'Dear Dad, the girls and I are having a great time.'

SC. 26   INT. CHINESE RESTAURANT – NIGHT

*Bill and family sit at a table in the Chinese restaurant. Leo Higgins
(from the opening wedding scene) is seated beside Bill. Perry is reading
out a postcard which shows a picture of the Hibiscus Island.*

> PERRY
> (*in a halting voice*)
> *Last night I sold a hundred dollars' worth of cosmetics to Barry
> Crocker – Muriel . . . PS   I am a fatso whale.

> BILL
> (*proudly, to Higgins*)
> *How 'bout that? A hundred dollars' worth to Barry Crocker.

> HIGGINS
> (*drunkenly slurring*)
> She's a great man, Bill. Like you.

*Amendment (28/10/93)

39

BETTY
*This cosmetics thing is the best thing that's ever happened to Muriel, it really is. She paid for this cruise herself, bought clothes to wear, new suitcases.

BILL
You listenin' to this, Perry?

Perry grunts.

BILL
Hey?

PERRY
I said yeah.

BILL
So you should be, you useless lump. Muriel's gone out and made somethin' of herself.

BETTY
(*trying to please*)
And she was more useless than anyone, wasn't she, Bill?

BILL
(*shakes his head*)
She's really impressed me. I told her that too. On the way to the airport for this holiday, I said you can't type but you've really impressed me.

HIGGINS
(*pointing to Bill*)
You know what they call this great man? Bill the Battler. 'Cause he's a little Aussie battler.

BILL
Been battlin' all me life.

HIGGINS
Battlin' for Porpoise Spit.

BILL
(*loudly in surprise*)
There's Deidre Chambers!

Everyone but Penelope turns to look at Deidre Chambers. Penelope is scratching the mosquito bites on her arm. She mouths 'What a coincidence' at the same time as Bill.

BILL
What a coincidence.
(*calls*)
Deidre! Deidre!

Deidre stops behind Penelope's chair. Penelope mops her bleeding bites with a serviette.

DEIDRE
(*surprised*)
Bill, hello. What a coincidence.

BILL
Take a seat. Penelope, shift over.

Penelope moves, but first deliberately drops her bloody serviette on to Deidre's seat. Deidre sits on it.

BILL
Deidre, Leo Higgins. He's concretin' Wallum Beach for us.
(*to Higgins*)
*Deidre got Muriel into this cosmetics thing. Perry, show Deidre Muriel's postcard.

Muriel's postcard is tossed on to the table before Deidre. She begins to read it.

BILL
*She's on Hibiscus Island. How 'bout that?

BETTY
She should really be sending you postcards, Deidre – you're the reason she's there.

Deidre, reading the postcard, looks very worried.

*Amendment (28/10/93)

41

At the cashier's counter, a small Chinese girl is attempting to get Bill to pay for the meal.

CHINESE GIRL
No, you have to pay. This is the bill . . .

BILL
It's all taken care of. Have a word to Charlie Chan over there.
                    (*calls*)
Charlie, Charlie . . .

CHINESE GIRL
(*bewildered*)
But you ate so much food . . .

BILL
Fix this lass up, will ya? She's confused.

A Chinese waiter takes the girl aside and they have a heated conversation in Chinese. Deidre, the bloodied serviette hanging off her bottom, approaches Bill.

DEIDRE
Bill . . .

BILL
(*low voice*)
I told you I was thinkin' about it.

DEIDRE
Not that. It's Muriel. In the past two weeks she's bought two kits from me at a cost of 40 dollars each. If she'd sold both kits for the recommended price she'd make 110 dollars, leaving her a profit of 30.30 dollars.

BILL
(*laughs*)
*What are you talkin' about? She's on a 3000-dollar holiday. She's makin' a fortune.
                    (*suddenly worried*)
Isn't she?
*Amendment (28/10/93)

Rhonda, sitting in a deck-chair on the deserted tropical beach, fills her glass with champagne from the giant bottle. Muriel, drunk and exultant, leans against a palm tree.

MURIEL

Do you think I could be famous?

RHONDA

Sure. For what?

MURIEL

I don't know. I could be an actress. I'm mental enough.

Rhonda begins 'Waterloo' again with a quick 'My My!' They sing the line, 'At Waterloo Napoleon did surrender' and end it on 'Oh, yeah!' Muriel sits in her deck-chair and looks up at the star-filled sky.

MURIEL
(*singing softly*)
'There was something in the air that night. The stars were bright.'

RHONDA

'Fernando.'

MURIEL and RHONDA
'They were shining there for you and me, for liberty, Fernando.'

RHONDA
'Though we never thought that we could lose, there's no regrets.'

MURIEL
'If I had to do the same again, I would my friend, Fernando'.

MURIEL and RHONDA
'If I had to do the same again, I would my friend, Fernando.'

RHONDA
(*laughs*)
They were the worst band in the world. I love them.

*Amendment (28/10/93)

The girls are quiet for a moment.

> MURIEL

Do you ever think you're nothing?

> RHONDA
> (*surprised*)

What?

> MURIEL

Sometimes I think I'm nothing.
> (*pause*)

Useless.

> RHONDA

You're not nothing, Muriel. You're amazing.

Muriel looks at Rhonda.

> RHONDA

Remember how you were in school? So quiet you could hardly talk. You were too shy to even look at people. You were at the bottom of the class in marks. You've come up from that to the top.

Muriel looks down.

> RHONDA

You're a success.
> (*excitedly*)

Someone wants to marry you. You're not nothing, Muriel. You've made it.

Muriel shrugs.

> RHONDA

Will you invite me to your wedding?

> MURIEL

I'll invite everyone.

Muriel looks ahead. The sky above the horizon line is turning orange in anticipation of sunrise.

MURIEL

I'll wear a white satin dress with lace bodice, pearl trims and a long train. I'll look so beautiful . . . they'll all be so jealous of me.

The sun rises, casting Muriel a brilliant orange.

MURIEL

It'll be the happiest day of my life.

SC. 28   INT. TAXI – DAY

Muriel, wearing a sarong, sunglasses and a tan, sits in the back of a taxi. Outside pass the sights of Porpoise Spit: pine trees, highrises, shopping malls, fun parks.

*From a Hibiscus Island bag crammed with souvenirs Muriel takes a colour photograph (taken by the resort photographer) showing a smiling Muriel and Rhonda seated in the resort restaurant.

Muriel smiles ruefully.

SC. 29   EXT. HESLOP HOUSE – DAY

The taxi drives up to the Heslop house. Cicadas buzz. Muriel climbs out of the car.

SC. 30   INT. HESLOP LOUNGEROOM/KITCHEN – DAY

Muriel walks up the stairs and into the loungeroom. Joan, wearing her Bill Heslop t-shirt, watches mid-day television; Betty stands motionless in the kitchen.

MURIEL

I'm back.

Betty gives a startled 'Oh'. Joan glares at Muriel.

JOAN

You're terrible, Muriel.

*Amendment (28/10/93)

45

BETTY

Muriel . . . Dad's so angry. He's coming back from the bank.

Muriel stiffens.

BETTY

He wants to talk to you. All our money's gone. Twelve
thousand dollars. You didn't do anything bad with those blank
cheques I gave you, did you? You wouldn't do that to me,
would you?

MURIEL

Course not.

*Muriel looks towards the verandah doors. The taxi is still parked in the
driveway. The driver is on the radio.*

Muriel picks up her suitcase and souvenirs and walks down the stairs.

*Betty moves to the glass doors and watches Muriel climb into the taxi.
The taxi drives off.*

SC. 31   INT. TAXI – DAY

Muriel, looking apprehensive, sits in the back seat.

*Through the windscreen she can see Bill's car approaching. She sinks
down in her seat as Bill races past the taxi.*

TAXI DRIVER

Where to, love?

SC. 32   TITLE CARD

A title card reads: CITY OF BRIDES

SC. 33   EXT. CITY OF SYDNEY – DAY

*Wide shot of the city of Sydney glinting in the morning sunshine. Camera
cranes down to a busy road in an inner-city suburb to reveal a small video
store.*

SC. 34   INT. VIDEO STORE – DAY

A monitor, perched high in a corner of the store, plays a video of the marriage of Prince Charles and Lady Diana. Through the front door of the store can be seen a giant billboard featuring a semi-naked muscular male model asleep in black satin sheets.

Muriel, seated behind a counter, watches the monitor. As Diana recites her vows, Muriel gazes at the billboard.

A young man, in his mid-twenties, enters the video store and walks to the new release section. This is Brice Nobes. He glances at Muriel.

Muriel glances at him and looks back at the monitor.

Brice selects a video and walks to the counter. He opens his mouth to speak but Muriel turns away, taking the video cover into a small room filled with shelves of video cassettes. Brice looks tense. Muriel returns to the counter. Brice smiles.

MURIEL

Card number?

BRICE

Ninety-two. Brice Nobes

Muriel enters the number into a small computer. Brice's file appears on screen and Muriel types in the cassette number.

MURIEL

You take out a lot of videos.

BRICE

Do I?

MURIEL

346 since August. You should join our Video Addicts Club. It's for people who take out too many videos.

BRICE

Too many?

MURIEL

You know, a lot. You get a dollar off every new release.

47

BRICE
(*nods*)

Do you want to go out with me?

MURIEL

What?

BRICE

You know . . . on a date.

MURIEL
(*after a moment, referring to the video box*)

Five dollars.

BRICE
(*taking money from his wallet*)

I was thinking maybe this Friday night . . .

Muriel places the money in a drawer.

BRICE

What do you say?

MURIEL
(*after a moment*)

You're not very . . .

BRICE

What?

Muriel hesitates.

BRICE

You can say it. I won't mind.

MURIEL

Handsome.

BRICE

Oh . . .
(*devastated*)

I didn't know you were gonna say that . . .
(*cheerfully*)

I'm funny, though. I make people laugh.

MURIEL

Why?

BRICE

I don't know. I'm an idiot, I s'pose.

Brice looks embarrassed. The telephone on the desk rings.

MURIEL
(*answers phone*)

Video Heaven.

SC. 35   INT. REJECT SHOP – DAY

Rhonda stands behind a counter in a Reject Shop (a discount outlet for flawed goods). She holds a small diary.

RHONDA

It's me. I still can't find any blokes for us tomorrow night. Even Tony's busy and his leg's in a cast.

MURIEL
(*looks at Brice, smiles*)

I've got one.

RHONDA
(*surprised*)

When did you do that?

MURIEL

Now.

RHONDA

You're racing off a customer? You've got the best job for
meeting men. Meet me for lunch. I want to hear every detail.

SC. 36   EXT. HAMBURGER BAR – DAY

*Muriel and Rhonda, eating hamburgers, sit at an outside table before a
small inner-city hamburger bar.*

RHONDA

I was getting worried about you. You've been in Sydney three
months and you haven't had it off with one guy. I thought you
might be pining for Tim.

MURIEL

Who?

RHONDA
(*shocked*)

Tim Simms. Your ex-fiancé. Have you even written to him yet?

MURIEL

I'm trying to forget him. This is my new life. I'm a new
person. I'm changing my name – to Mariel.

RHONDA

That is your name.

MURIEL

Mariel.

(*spells it out*)

M.A.R.I.E.L.

RHONDA

(*pause*)

Muriel . . .

MURIEL

Mariel.

RHONDA

Mariel . . . are you on the run from the law?

MURIEL

(*shocked*)

What? No.

RHONDA

I don't care if you are, I'd just like to know.

MURIEL

(*after a moment's thought*)

You know Tim?

Rhonda nods.

MURIEL

He was a policeman.

RHONDA

You jilted a cop?

Muriel nods.

RHONDA

(*dramatically*)

He's after you.

MURIEL

He said if ever I left him he'd find out who I was living with and shoot them. Then he'd shoot me, then himself.

RHONDA

Don't write to him yet. I wouldn't even call your family for a while.

MURIEL
(*with a small smile*)

I won't.

RHONDA

Shit. He really loved you, didn't he?

SC. 37   INT. BRICE'S CAR – NIGHT

Brice's car moves through the Saturday night city traffic. Muriel, wearing a tightly fitting black stretch-knit blouse (which has a zip up the middle), black leather pants and sunglasses, sits in the passenger seat smoking a cigarette. She smiles at Brice.

Brice, looking tense, returns the smile and looks back at the road.

Rhonda, drinking from a bottle of beer, leans over the back seat.

RHONDA

So, Brice, what do you do for a living?

BRICE

I'm a parking inspector.

Muriel and Rhonda stare at Brice.

SC. 38   INT. NIGHTCLUB – NIGHT

In a brackishly lit nightclub, Rhonda dances sensuously with two sailors (both in full uniform). Muriel and Brice sit in a side booth near the dance floor.

MURIEL
(*loudly over the music*)

Rhonda changed my life.

BRICE

She would. Do you want to go somewhere else?

MURIEL

Rhonda wants to stay here.

Rhonda, flushed from her exertions, arrives at the booth.

RHONDA

I'm going. I've got a date.

The two sweaty sailors, smiles on their faces, wait by the dance floor.

RHONDA
(*excitedly*)

They're American.

(*picks up her coat*)
Have fun. Don't do anything I wouldn't do.

Rhonda leaves with the sailors. Muriel looks at Brice.

MURIEL

Do you want to dance?

BRICE

I'm a terrible dancer.

                          MURIEL
I don't care.

*Muriel and Brice move to the dance floor. They begin to dance
awkwardly to the music. Brice is a terrible dancer.*

SC. 39   EXT. CITY – NIGHT

Muriel and Brice walk down a city street.

                          BRICE
Rhonda said you were engaged. What was he like? Your fiancé?

                          MURIEL
Like . . .
                       (*looks up*)
                          him.

*Above them, on the wall of a building, is a billboard featuring the male
model asleep in his sheets.*

                          BRICE
                       (*dismayed*)
Why didn't you marry him?

                          MURIEL
I couldn't. If you'd known me in Porpoise Spit you wouldn't
think I was me now.

                          BRICE
What were you like in Porpoise Spit?

                          MURIEL
I'm not like that any more. I'm almost a new person.

                          BRICE
When will you be finished?

                          MURIEL
I don't know.

*They stop before a low stone wall that overlooks the harbour. A riverboat
party glides by. Couples dance to the tune of Lai's 'A Man and a*

Woman'. *On the stern a silhouetted couple are in passionate embrace.*
Muriel looks at Brice.

MURIEL

I need experiences. I don't have any.

BRICE

Me either. Maybe we need the same ones.
(*pause*)
Why don't we go back to your place?

SC. 40   INT. FLAT – NIGHT

*Muriel and Brice enter a white-walled, sparsely furnished flat. There is a
fold-out chair, a beanbag, a television set and an empty birdcage hanging
on a metal stand. On the wall are air-brushed poster prints of Abba,
Elvis, James Dean and Marilyn Monroe, and numerous polaroid photos
showing Muriel and Rhonda drunk at parties. There is a small verandah
with a view of the city.*

*Rhonda's and the two sailors' clothing is distributed around the room.
There is the sound of raucous laughter coming from Rhonda's bedroom.*

BRICE

Nice flat. Very . . . spacious.

*Muriel enters the kitchen, plugs in the jug and takes two mugs from the
cupboard. Brice hovers in the doorway of the kitchen. The sounds from
the bedroom are clearly affecting him.*

BRICE

Black . . . no sugar.

*One of the men in Rhonda's bedroom begins to bark like a dog. Rhonda
screams with laughter. Both men begin to bark. There is the sound of bed
springs creaking and a head-board banging on a wall. Rhonda and the
men start groaning.*

MURIEL

Bikkies?

What? Sure.

*Muriel empties a packet of biscuits on to a paper plate. The groaning
becomes louder, more passionate. Muriel pours hot water into the mugs.
They enter the loungeroom.*

*Muriel switches on the television with a remote control. A news break
shows footage of a hurricane devastating Hibiscus Island.*

NEWSREADER'S VOICE
*In tonight's news, holidaymakers and staff airlifted to safety as
Cyclone Terry devastates the Hibiscus Island resort.

*Muriel sits into the beanbag. Brice sits beside her. Air hisses from the
beanbag.*

NEWSREADER'S VOICE
*Buildings and vegetation were flattened in minutes by winds of
more than 160 kilometres per hour . . .

MURIEL
*Rhonda and I went on that island.

BRICE
(*totally uninterested*)

Looks like fun.

*The groaning from the bedroom increases in intensity. Brice shifts his
position and his body presses against Muriel.*

MURIEL
(*offering plate of biscuits*)

Tim-tam?

BRICE

Maybe after.

(*quickly*)

Later.

Muriel sets down the plate. During all this we hear:

*Amendment (28/10/93)

57

The Government Inquiry into corruption on the North Coast
continued today with President of the Porpoise Spit Council,
Bill Heslop, admitting that he received secret payments from a
Japanese land developer. Councillor Heslop said his judgement
had been impaired by the shock disappearance of his daughter
and made this emotional plea outside the Inquiry building . . .

Brice looks at Muriel.

BRICE

Mariel . . . ?

BILL'S VOICE

Muriel . . .

MURIEL

Mariel.

BILL'S VOICE

Muriel . . .

BRICE

What?

Muriel looks towards the television.

On screen is Bill surrounded by microphones and cameras.

BILL
(*directly into camera*)
. . . if you're watchin' this, we just wanna know you're alright. We
don't care about the money, we just wanna know you're
alright . . .

*Muriel is horrified and changes the channel by remote. Bill is replaced by
a hot sex scene in a music video. Muriel looks at Brice. He leans in and
kisses her. Muriel stifles a nervous giggle.*

*Brice straddles Muriel, pushing her body down into the hissing beanbag.
He begins to kiss her neck, while his hand kneads her body through her
clothing. A giggle escapes from Muriel. Rhonda and the sailors continue
to moan.*

Brice kneels and looks down at Muriel, who lies still on the beanbag.

BRICE

I'm sorry I'm a parking inspector.

MURIEL

That's okay . . .

Brice pulls off his coat. His fingers take hold of the metal ring at the top of the zip on Muriel's stretch-knit blouse. He pulls it, but the zip is stuck. He pulls it again – no go. He yanks hard and the zip flies open. Muriel gives an undignified hoot.

Brice stares at Muriel's breasts (cupped in a black bra) like a man possessed. He kisses her bra, breasts and stomach. Muriel giggles uncontrollably, her hands moving skittishly over her torso in a vague attempt at modesty.

Brice tries to open the blouse completely, but the zip is jammed half-way. He tries to pull the blouse up over Muriel's head, but it bunches up around her torso. Muriel hoots with laughter. His hands move to the heavy belt that buckles Muriel's leather pants. He opens the belt and unzips the pants. The sailors and Rhonda are reaching mutual orgasm.

Brice begins to furiously tug the pants down over Muriel's ample thighs. They are stuck fast. He pulls a vertical running zip on Muriel's right thigh, and reaches for the identical zip on the left thigh. His fingers take hold of the beanbag zipper and pull. The side of the beanbag gapes open. Brice grips the pants and yanks hard. Muriel whoops as she slides from the beanbag to the floor. Small white foam balls erupt from the beanbag and spread across the carpet. Bill appears on the television again in another newsbreak. Muriel, aghast, gropes for the remote control.

BILL

(*tersely, to the press*)

*They weren't bribes, they were commissions from Japanese mates. A bribe's someone payin' you to do a favour, a commission's a way of sayin' thanks when a favour's done. Now . . . I might get a bit emotional on this next bit . . . You listenin'?

Brice, red-faced with exertion and passion, crouches over Muriel and tugs

*Amendment (28/10/93)

59

on her pants. Muriel attempts to change channels with a tim-tam. She discards it and finds the remote.

BILL

*Me family and I suffered a personal tragedy . . . me oldest daughter Muriel stole 12,000 from me bank account and disappeared, forcin' me to accept commissions for favours I otherwise woulda done as favours . . .

The channel changes to show more footage of Bill.

BILL

. . . Muriel, if you're watchin' this, we just wanna know you're alright. We don't care about the money . . .

Muriel jams the remote again. The volume increases, but the channel stays the same. In the bedroom, Rhonda and the sailors are loudly coming.

Brice pulls with all his might. The pants suddenly disgorge Muriel's thighs and Brice flies backwards into the air, slamming into the empty birdcage. The stand crashes through the glass doors that lead on to the verandah. The curtains fall from above the doors and entangle Brice. Wind gusts into the loungeroom and the white foam balls fly about the room.

On the television the Aquamaid sinks again at an amplified volume.

Rhonda's bedroom door bursts open and two naked sailors run into the loungeroom. They see Muriel lying on the floor, her pants down, her blouse bunched up and around her middle. She is giggling, apparently hysterical.

Brice fights his way out of the curtains. One of the enraged naked sailors leaps on to Brice and wrestles him to the floor. Brice, stunned, calls for help.

SECOND SAILOR

What'd you do to her?

BRICE

Nothing! I . . . I . . .

*Amendment (28/10/93)

60

The first naked sailor stands over Muriel.

FIRST SAILOR

Are you alright?

Muriel, eye level with his genitals, screams with laughter.

An old woman, standing on a verandah on the opposite block of flats, begins to scream as she sees Brice and Muriel being attacked by two burly nude men.

Rhonda, wearing a dressing gown, runs into the room.

RHONDA

What's going on?

Brice is waving a chequebook.

BRICE

I'll write a cheque for the door! I'll write a cheque!

Muriel laughs hysterically. Rhonda begins to laugh. Her laughter builds, and soon she is roaring with Muriel. She slides down the wall to the floor.

The First Sailor relinquishes Brice, who starts writing out a cheque.

Laughing, leaning against the wall, Rhonda looks at Muriel.

RHONDA

Mariel . . . I can't move my legs.

SC. 41   EXT. STREET – NIGHT

An ambulance roars up a city road.

SC. 42   INT. HOSPITAL CASUALTY – NIGHT

In the hospital emergency waiting-room Muriel sits on a moulded plastic chair by the door. At the end of the corridor a cleaning vehicle with yellow flashing lights moves across the polished tile floor.

Muriel waits. Outside the glass doors dawn has broken. Muriel looks towards a red phone that sits in a corner of the room. She looks through her purse for change.

SC. 43   INT. HESLOP BEDROOM – DAY

In Bill and Betty's bedroom the phone on Bill's desk rings. Through the window a new highrise blocks the view of the ocean. Joan enters and answers the phone.

JOAN

Hullo?

(pause. No reply)

Hullo?

MURIEL

It's me. Muriel.

JOAN

You're terrible, Muriel.

MURIEL

Why's Dad on TV?

JOAN

The Inquiry. They're sayin' he takes bribes.

MURIEL

Does he?

JOAN

Yeah, but he had to 'cause you stole all our money.

(softer voice)

Dad's moved out. He says it's all Mum's fault 'cause she gave you the cheques. He's living in a hotel.

Betty appears in the doorway of the bedroom.

BETTY

(an hysterical edge in her voice)

Who is it? Is it Dad?

JOAN

Muriel

Muriel? Oh . . . oh . . . oh . . .

Betty totters into the bedroom reaching for the phone.

JOAN
(into phone)

Mum wants to talk to you.

BETTY
(takes phone)

Muriel . . . Are you alright? We didn't know what had happened
to you. We thought you'd become a prostitute or a drug addict.

MURIEL

I'm in Sydney.

BETTY

Dad's in Sydney for the Inquiry. He'd love to see you. Where
are you staying?

Muriel remains silent.

BETTY

He just wants to know you're alright.

MURIEL

Joan said he's moved out.

BETTY

No. Well . . . yes, but only for his health. Doctor Farrell says
he needs a holiday from us . . . Oh . . . I know he blames me
for you taking the money, but I never thought you'd do
anything like that.
(hopefully)
Maybe there was some sort of mistake at the bank . . . or I wrote
the wrong figure on the cheque . . .

MURIEL

No. I took it.

Malcolm appears in the doorway.

MALCOLM

Mum, the Federal Police are here!

BETTY

Oh . . . I have to go, we're being raided again. What's your phone number?

The sound of heavy knocking at the back door and footsteps on the loungeroom stairs.

MURIEL

I don't have a phone.

BETTY

What's your address?

MURIEL

I'll call you later.

BETTY

Ring Dad. He's at the Hilton.

Four hard-faced men in suits stride into the bedroom. One of the men begins to search Bill's desk, another a cupboard.

FIRST MAN

Mrs Heslop, don't lie to us, we know everything.

A female stenographer sits on the end of the bed and flips open a portable word-processor.

FIRST MAN

We want to ask you some questions about Bill.

SC. 44   INT. HOSPITAL CORRIDOR – DAY

A sign on the ceiling reads: 'Neurosurgery Ward'

DOCTOR DRISCOLL'S VOICE

The brain is the engine room and travelling down the spinal cord . . .

Doctor Driscoll, in his early fifties, sits on the side of Rhonda's bed holding up an x-ray. Rhonda wears a hospital gown. Muriel sits in a bedside chair.

                    DRISCOLL
          (*his finger moving down the spine on the x-ray*)
. . . are electrical wires, if you like, peeling off at every level, sending the brain's orders to the body.

His finger reaches the small dark shadow (about the size of a cherry) located on the spine in the lumbar region.

                    DRISCOLL
This tumour is pressing on the spinal cord interrupting the flow of electricity to your legs.
                    (*sets aside x-ray*)
The operation will remove that pressure. I'd like to do it soon, in the next 24 hours.

                    RHONDA
How did I get it? I mean . . . it's nothing to do with too much sex is it?

                    DRISCOLL
                    (*smiles*)
No. Nothing like that.

Rhonda looks relieved.

                    DRISCOLL
We don't know what causes cancer.

                    RHONDA
                    (*shocked*)
Cancer?

                    MURIEL
Cancer?

                    RHONDA
You never said anything about cancer.

DRISCOLL
(*uncomfortable*)
That's what the tumour is – it's a cancer.

RHONDA
(*loudly*)
I've got cancer?
(*throws her head back*)
Oh God! I'm going to go bald and have to eat macrobiotic food!

MURIEL
You said it was electrical.

DRISCOLL
(*answering Rhonda*)
We're not talking about radio therapy. This is a discrete tumour –
alone, isolated. The operation's all we need for the moment.

RHONDA
For the moment?

DRISCOLL
There's always the possibility that it could be a malignant
tumour.

MURIEL
What's that mean?

RHONDA
It means I'm up shit creek, that's what it means.

SC. 46   EXT. INNER-CITY STREET – DAY

*Muriel, looking dazed, walks down an inner-city street. She passes a
bridal wear shop. Mannequin brides, their arms outstretched, fingers
beckoning, look out at her from the shop window. A sign reads:
Cinderella's Bridal Wear. Muriel enters the shop.*

SC. 47   INT. BRIDAL WEAR SHOP – DAY

The shop is pink and mauve, with white wedding dresses hanging on racks. In a far corner is a small platform facing three full-length mirrors. Muriel is drawn to a mannequin wearing a white silk dress. She gently takes the fabric of the billowing skirt between her fingers.

A middle-aged Manageress moves up behind Muriel.

>   MANAGERESS
> Silk Chantel. Imported. When's your big day.

Muriel looks at the Manageress.

>   MANAGERESS
> Your wedding day?

>   MURIEL
> September.

>   MANAGERESS
>   (*pleased*)
> Spring. Ivory.

Close-up of the Manageress's hands taking an ivory-coloured wedding dress from a rack. She displays it over her forearm. Muriel looks down at the dress.

>   MANAGERESS
> Would you like to try it on?

Fingers button up the back of the dress.

Hands spread a wide train out across the platform.

A tulle veil is fixed on to Muriel's head.

The Manageress and her assistant step back.

Muriel, dressed as a bride, turns to face the mirrors. The effect is stunning. Muriel's eyes are filled with awe. She slowly lifts her veil. The Manageress fusses with the dress.

>   MANAGERESS
> What's your fiancé's name?

MURIEL
(*after a moment*)

Bill.

MANAGERESS

Bill's in for a big surprise. Will your mother be coming in to
see the dress?

MURIEL

No. She can't. She's in hospital.

The Manageress and the assistant look concerned.

MURIEL

She's got a tumour on her spine. She has to have an operation.

The Manageress looks moved. She crosses to a desk.

MANAGERESS

We don't usually do this, but your mother has to see how
beautiful you look in this dress.

*The Manageress takes a polaroid camera from a drawer. The assistant
impulsively takes a single white lily from a vase and places it in Muriel's
hands.*

*Holding the lily like a bouquet, Muriel smiles into the camera and the
Manageress takes her picture.*

SC. 48   INT. FLAT – DAY

*Muriel's hands tear off the plastic that covers a new white wedding
album. Gold embossed lettering on the cover reads: Our Wedding Day.*

*She sits on the floor of the loungeroom. Sunshine glints off the shards of
broken glass scattered around her and a breeze through the shattered
verandah doors billows the curtains. Her fingers peel back the transparent
adhesive plastic on the first page of the album. She carefully mounts four
polaroid photographs showing her in the wedding dress.*

Muriel smooths down the plastic and admires the photos.

68

Rhonda's mother, Berris, dressed in her trip-to-the-city best, is a tall, tense woman of fifty who hides her anxiety about everything underneath a faux cheerfulness. She stands at the end of Rhonda's hospital bed. Rhonda's bare feet, resting on a pillow, poke out from beneath the sheets. Muriel stands beside Rhonda.

> BERRIS

I'm going to stay here till you're all better.

> RHONDA
> (*appalled*)

That could be months, Mum.

> BERRIS

Till your toes move then.
> (*sits in chair beside bed*)

I don't care how long it takes, Rhonda, my place is with you. And maybe I'll get to see some of Sydney while I'm here. You and Mariel can tell me where to go.

Rhonda cocks an eyebrow and looks at Muriel.

> BERRIS

Now . . . what went wrong with this operation?

> RHONDA

It was bigger than they thought, and it wasn't pressing on my spinal cord like they thought, it was growing out of it. So when they cut it out they had to cut some nerves.

> BERRIS
> (*quickly, neurotically*)

I'm sure everything will be fine. Just fine.

She rummages through her handbag and takes out some photos.

> BERRIS

I brought you some pictures of Porpoise Spit.

Two bedridden elderly ladies, who share Rhonda's room, exchange disturbed looks.

RHONDA
(*to old ladies*)

Don't worry, it's a town.

BERRIS

It's changed so much. There's Waterworld . . . those new
highrises on the beachfront . . . Dreamland . . .

Berris starts to cry. Rhonda sighs.

BERRIS

I'm sorry . . . it's the way you live that's caused this . . . if
you'd stayed home in Porpoise Spit none of this would be
happening.

RHONDA

No, because I would've shot myself.

BERRIS

I'm the only one of my friends who isn't a grandmother.
(*regains control, sniffs*)
If the worst does happen, I'm taking you home.

RHONDA

Forget it, Mum.

BERRIS

How do you expect to cope by yourself in a wheelchair?

MURIEL

She won't be by herself, she'll be with me.

RHONDA

And I'm not going to be in a wheelchair for long. I'm going to
walk.

BERRIS
(*a new tack*)

You won't be going back to work for a while. How will you pay
rent?

RHONDA

I'll get on the invalid pension.

MURIEL

And I don't mind paying a bit more.

BERRIS

What about those stairs up to your flat?

RHONDA

I'll drag myself. I've still got arms.

BERRIS

Your wheelchair . . . ?

MURIEL
(*quickly*)

I'll carry it.

BERRIS

Alright, Mariel: what happens when it's three o'clock in the morning and Rhonda falls off the toilet?

Muriel and Rhonda stare at Berris, look at each other and burst into laughter. Berris looks indignant. As Rhonda laughs, her toes twitch. Muriel notices immediately.

MURIEL

Your toes moved.

Rhonda's laughter subsides.

RHONDA

What?

MURIEL
(*excited*)

Your toes moved!

Rhonda looks down at her toes and wiggles them.

RHONDA
(*screams*)

My toes moved! I can move my toes!

Muriel shrieks with excitement.

RHONDA

Call someone! Call the nurses! My toes are moving!

Muriel presses the bedside buzzer. Berris looks bemused.

BERRIS

What does this mean?

SC. 50   EXT. HOSPITAL – DAY

Berris, dressed in her best leaving-the-city clothes, stands beside a taxi parked before the hospital. Rhonda, seated in a wheelchair, and Muriel are on the footpath.

BERRIS

I didn't get to see any of Sydney.

She climbs into the back of the taxi and looks miserable as it drives away. Muriel and Rhonda wave goodbye.

RHONDA

Promise me something? Whatever happens . . . I can't go back to Porpoise Spit. I want to stay here in Sydney.

MURIEL

Your toes moved. You're going to walk.

RHONDA

Promise.

MURIEL

I promise.

Muriel wheels Rhonda back to the hospital.

MURIEL

You're going to walk.

SC. 51   INT. REHABILITATION CENTRE – DAY

In a sun-filled gym in the rehabilitation centre Rhonda is working on the parallel rails under the supervision of a thickset female physiotherapist.

72

Muriel walks alongside Rhonda. Rhonda is finding each step both strenuous and painful.

PHYSIO

You're doing well . . . Isn't she doing well, Mariel?

MURIEL
(*with a pained expression*)
You're doing really well.

PHYSIO
(*talking over Muriel*)
Move that foot forward. You can do it . . .

Rhonda grimaces in pain as her right foot slowly moves forward.

PHYSIO

Good, good. Now the other . . .

RHONDA

I have to sit down . . . I have to sit down.

The Physio and Muriel help Rhonda into her wheelchair. Rhonda, exhausted and stressed, bursts into tears. She covers her face with her hands.

PHYSIO

Take a break, honey. You're doing really well.

The Physio moves off. Muriel kneels beside Rhonda's chair. Rhonda wipes her nose with a tissue.

RHONDA

How can you stand this? All I do is cry. I'm like a baby. You push me around in this chair, you cook for me, you even help me dress. I hate it. I don't hate it . . . I hate that you have to do it.

When I lived in Porpoise Spit I'd stay in my room for hours
and listen to Abba songs. Sometimes I'd stay in there all day.
Since I met you and moved to Sydney, I haven't listened to one
Abba song. It's because now my life's as good as an Abba song,
as good as 'Dancing Queen'.

RHONDA
(*touched in spite of herself*)

Come off it.

Rhonda looks at Muriel.

RHONDA
(*sniffs, wipes her eyes*)

Call back Mrs Himmler.

Muriel smiles and looks across the gym to the Physio.

MURIEL
(*calls*)

Mrs Himmler! She wants to start, again.

Rhonda bursts into laughter. Muriel looks confused.

SC. 54   INT. FLAT – DAY

*Rhonda sits in the loungeroom watching mid-day television. There is a
knock at the door. Rhonda opens it.*

TAXI DRIVER

Taxi for the rehabilitation centre?

RHONDA

That's me. Hang on, I want to get my smokes.

*Rhonda switches off the TV and wheels into her bedroom. She takes a
cigarette packet from her bedside table. It is empty. She moves to Muriel's
bedroom and opens a cupboard, revealing a small carton of cigarettes.
She takes out a full packet and turns for the door. She stops.*

Hidden behind the door is Muriel's photo album. The cover inscription clearly reads 'Our Wedding Day'.

Rhonda picks up the album and opens it. On the first pages are eight polaroid photos of Muriel modelling a pair of wedding dresses.

Rhonda, surprised, turns the page to find eight more photos of Muriel in two more dresses.

She rapidly flips through the album, revealing page after page of photos of Muriel wearing dresses of different styles, colours and costs. Both cheap and expensive stores are represented. In all photos Muriel has the same look of misty-eyed satisfaction.

SC. 55   INT. VIDEO STORE – DAY

Muriel's finger travels down the bridal wear column in the Yellow Pages and stops beside a store in a nearby suburb. Muriel circles the address with a marker pen. A number of other addresses have been circled and crossed out.

Muriel takes a polaroid camera from behind her counter. It is the same camera she bought on the cruise.

SC. 56   EXT. VIDEO STORE – DAY

Muriel closes the door of the video store and walks up the street towards a bus stop. She passes a small bridal wear store. She stops and gazes at the mannequin bride in the window. Muriel looks about and enters the store.

SC. 57   INT. TAXI – DAY

Rhonda sits in the back of the taxi.

> RHONDA
> (*to driver*)
Slow down before this video store.

A sign in the door of Video Heaven reads: 'Back in Ten Minutes'.

> RHONDA
> (*dismayed*)

Keep going.

The taxi accelerates. Rhonda looks out her window.

To glimpse Muriel, through the doorway of the small bridal store, outfitted in a flowing white bridal gown.

> RHONDA

Stop the car!

SC. 58   INT. BRIDAL STORE #2 — DAY

In the bridal store the Manageress and her assistant admire Muriel's dress.

> MANAGERESS #2

Beautiful. I hope the photos help your sister out of that coma.

The Manageress aims the polaroid camera. Muriel poses.

> MURIEL

She might wake up to look at them.

> RHONDA

Mariel!

Muriel screams, whirls around to find Rhonda in the store.

> RHONDA

What are you doing?

> MURIEL
> (*in a panic*)

Nothing!

Rhonda wheels towards Muriel.

> RHONDA

Why didn't you tell me you were going to marry Tim?

MURIEL
(*edging back*)

Who?

RHONDA

Tim Simms! Your fiancé! The one who wants to shoot you!

The Manageress steps in.

MANAGERESS #2

Just a minute! You can't come in here and threaten brides. I
don't care how unfortunate you are.

RHONDA

Oh, fuck off!

*The Manageress gasps. Muriel retreats into a back storeroom. Rhonda
follows, cornering Muriel amongst dismembered mannequins and old and
unfinished dresses.*

RHONDA

What's going on, Mariel? I've seen your wedding album –
you've tried on every wedding dress in Sydney.

MURIEL

That doesn't mean I'm getting married.

RHONDA

What else does it mean?

MURIEL

I want to get married. I've always wanted to get married. If I
can get married it means I've changed, I'm a new person.

RHONDA

How?

MURIEL

Because who'd want to marry me?

RHONDA
(*not so sure any more*)

Tim Simms.

77

MURIEL

There isn't any Tim Simms! I made him up!

There is a growing passion in Muriel's voice.

MURIEL

In Porpoise Spit no one would even look at me. But when I came to Sydney and became Mariel, Brice asked me out. That proves I'm already different than I was.
(*triumphantly*)
And if someone wants to marry me I'm not her any more. I'm me.

RHONDA

Her?

MURIEL
(*spits it out*)
Muriel! Muriel Heslop! Stupid, fat and useless! I hate her! I'm not going back to being her again!

Muriel slumps miserably into a corner.

MURIEL

Why can't it be me? Why can't I be the one?

Rhonda stares at Muriel. The Manageress leans into Rhonda.

MANAGERESS #2

Have you been in a coma?

Rhonda turns and wheels out of the store.

SC. 59   INT. VIDEO STORE – DAY

Muriel, in casual clothes, enters the video store. Outside workmen paste a new poster over the billboard of the sleeping male model. The new poster shows a scrubbed young couple happy about their first home loan. Muriel stands behind the counter. The phone rings. She grabs it up.

78

(*hopefully*)

Rhonda?

(*pause*)

Dad.

SC. 60   INT. CHINESE RESTAURANT IN CITY – DAY

Bill sits at a table in an inner-city Chinese restaurant. With him are his barrister and two solicitors. Muriel enters the restaurant and walks to Bill's table.

BILL

Muriel! Where's that money?

MURIEL

I spent it.

BILL

Why'd you do it to me? I gave ya money, got ya jobs.
(*to lawyers*)
I put her through this secretarial course. Cost me two thousand dollars for two years, she comes out an' she can't even type.

Muriel, squirming with embarrassment, sits beside the lawyers.

BILL

I get 'er into sellin' cosmetics. We all think she's makin' a go of it, turns out she's robbin' us blind.
(*to Muriel*)
You're a disgrace. An absolute disgrace.

A small boy of eight approaches Bill.

BOY

Are you Bill the battler? I've seen you on TV.
(*holds out paper and pen*)
Can I have your autograph?

BILL
(*pleased*)

What's your name?

79

BOY

Judd Piper.

BILL

Ya play footy, Judd?

Judd nods.

BILL

What team ya barrack for?

BOY

*The Bulldogs.

MURIEL

I've changed my name . . . to Mariel.

BOY
(*taking autograph*)
My Dad and I think you're not guilty, Bill.

BILL

Good on ya. Spread it around.

BOY
(*runs off*)
You can't stop progress!

BILL
(*to Muriel*)
You're comin' back to Porpoise Spit with me.

Muriel looks horrified.

BILL

We'll be goin' in three weeks once this Inquiry crap's over.

MURIEL

I can't go back. I'm a new person.

BILL

You're a thief. The only reason I didn't get the cops on to you is your Mum begged me not to. I want that money back. I'll get you a job at the Leagues Club and arrange you a bank loan. You're gonna make up for what you done, Muriel.

(*in surprise*)

There's Deidre Chambers!

Deidre Chambers, dressed beautifully, stands in the entrance of the restaurant waiting for a table.

BILL
(*calling*)

Deidre! Deidre!

DEIDRE
(*feigning surprise*)

Bill!

BILL

What a coincidence. What are you doing in Sydney?

DEIDRE

My sister lives here. I'm down for the long weekend.
(*over Bill's next line*)

What a coincidence . . .

BILL

Pull up a chair. Deidre, me barrister: Graham Newnham, his two solicitors. Muriel you know about.

MURIEL
(*loud*)

It's Mariel!

An embarrassed pause.

BARRISTER

We should get back, Bill. Victor Keinosuke's testimony starts at two . . .

BILL

The Jap bastard.

(*to Muriel*)

He's gonna testify I took bribes from him.

DEIDRE

Commissions.

BILL

I took commissions. I cut through all that red tape for 'em, I deserved some sort of acknowledgement. They'd never 'ave got to build that resort on Crown land without me.

DEIDRE

It was the Crown land that did it.

BILL

Total over-reaction.

DEIDRE

Aboriginals lived on it.

BILL

I promised 'em Housing Commission flats.

DEIDRE

Which were perfectly nice. They were living in sheds . . . and the way the women dress . . .

BILL

They wrote to the bloody greenie politicians, demanded an Inquiry. The house was raided by the Federal Police. Ya Mum let 'em walk right in. She an' Perry gave 'em statements – told 'em I 'ad money problems!

DEIDRE

Don't think about it.

BILL

Course I 'ad money problems,

(*indicating Muriel*)

she stole most of it.

Deidre places a comforting hand on Bill's hand.

> DEIDRE
>
> You need your family around you now, Bill.

> BILL
> *(points at Muriel)*
>
> If the Feds come an' see you, don't say a word.

> MURIEL
>
> Are you and Deidre together?

> BILL
> *(pause)*
>
> What?

> MURIEL
>
> Have you left Mum for Deidre?

> DEIDRE
>
> Yes. We're in love.

Deidre takes Bill's hand. Bill looks uncomfortable.

> MURIEL
>
> What about Mum?

Bill looks away.

> DEIDRE
>
> What happiness has your father had in his life if he doesn't have me?

Bill continues to avoid Muriel's look.

> MURIEL
>
> What about Mum?

Bill looks at Muriel.

> BILL
>
> She'll have you. You got three weeks.

SC. 61   INT. STAIRWELL OF FLAT – NIGHT

Muriel trudges up the stairwell to the flat.

SC. 62   INT. FLAT – NIGHT

The loungeroom is dark. Rhonda is silhouetted before the verandah doors.
Muriel turns on the light. Rhonda has been crying.

RHONDA
It's come back. The tumour.
(*pause*)
I've been having back pains. I didn't tell you 'cause I thought
they'd go away. Anyway, they gave me an x-ray, then a
myelogram. It's come back and I have to have another operation.
I'm not going to walk.

MURIEL
But . . . what about your rehabilitation.

RHONDA
They're going to cut my spinal cord, Mariel.
(*pause*)
Mum called. She wants to take me back to Porpoise Spit.

MURIEL
When?

RHONDA
(*surprised*)
I'm not going. I told her I'm staying here with you.

Muriel walks to her bedroom. Rhonda wheels into the doorway.

RHONDA
We're going to stick together, aren't we, Muriel? You
promised.

Muriel nods.

MURIEL

Course.

(*pause*)

I just . . . I always thought you'd walk.

Rhonda looks at Muriel. Muriel looks away.

SC. 63   INT. VIDEO STORE – DAY

Muriel leafs through a copy of a magazine called Single in Sydney. *Her finger stops beside an ad that reads: Wife wanted.*

She picks up the phone and dials the number printed with the ad. After a few rings a gruff male voice answers.

VOICE

City baths.

Muriel hangs up. She checks the number and dials again.

VOICE

City baths.

MURIEL

Um . . . I'm ringing about the ad, about the wife.

VOICE

Oh, yeah. Just let me close the door of me office.

(*pause*)

Who am I talkin' to?

SC. 64   INT. CITY BATHS – DAY

Muriel enters the main pool area of the city baths. A ruddy-faced coach, in his mid-forties, shouts instructions to a squad of swimmers doing laps in the Olympic pool. Muriel stands behind the coach. He turns.

KEN

Mariel?

Muriel nods. Ken vigorously shakes her hand.

KEN

Ken Blundell. How are ya?
> (*indicating a grandstand*)

Let's go over here so we can talk.

Ken sits on the grandstand beside Muriel.

KEN

So . . .
> (*pause*)

You do any swimmin'?

MURIEL
> (*worried*)

What? No.

KEN

Are you broadminded?

MURIEL
> (*pause*)

I live in Newtown.
> (*then, with barely concealed repulsion*)

Will I be marrying you?

KEN
> (*with a smile*)

No.

Ken goes to the side of the pool.

KEN
> (*shouts*)

Van Arckle!

A young man of twenty climbs out of the water. He is handsome and blond, with a magnificent physique. He picks up a towel and approaches Muriel.

KEN

David Van Arckle, Mariel Heslop.

Muriel, awestruck, stares up at this arrogant young god. David looks

Muriel over as he would a used car he is considering buying. He takes a seat on the grandstand. Ken sits beside him. As Ken talks, Muriel stares at David.

KEN

Mariel, you've probably seen the news about the civil war in South Africa. Just as it looked like the South Africans were doing the right things by their blacks, makin' reforms, the police go an' open fire on a black soccer club. Which is bad news for David.

MURIEL
(*to David*)

Are you black?

DAVID
(*in a South African accent*)

What?

Muriel pulls a face.

MURIEL

I don't know why I said that.

Muriel giggles with embarrassment.

David, incredulous, stares at Muriel.

Which only increases her discomfort. She guffaws and pulls another face.

KEN

I suppose it is funny in a way. They get back into the world's sportin' events and just as young David's ready to go they muck it up and they're out again. But let's be honest, the South Africans were never much chop in the pool. David here's a bit of a freak, really.

Muriel stifles a giggle.

KEN

*He's one of the best freestyle swimmers I've ever seen, and I think he could take gold in the 1500 metres in the next Olympic Games.

Muriel pokes her tongue out and pulls another face. David stares at her.

KEN

*Mariel, how did you feel when Kieran Perkins took gold for Australia in Barcelona?

MURIEL

Who?

DAVID
(*shocked*)

*Kieran Perkins. He's an Australian champion.

*Amendment (28/10/93)

KEN

What I'm saying, Mariel, is this is your chance to do something
for Australian sport. Dave's family will do anything to see him
fulfil his potential as a champion, even if it means him
competin' for another country. They're willin' to pay 10,000
dollars to the girl who can help Dave out.

(pause)

Are you from Sydney originally?

MURIEL

What? No. Porpoise Spit.

KEN

Why'd you leave there?

MURIEL

Well . . . Because of all the mental things that happened to me,
I got shallow. And my physical being could have been
improved and as well as my mentality.

DAVID
(carefully)

Are you alright now?

KEN

I don't think Mariel meant . . . being mental, as in mad.

MURIEL

What? No.

Muriel begins to giggle.

KEN

You mean your sense of self.

Muriel nods.

MURIEL

My mental identity.

Muriel pulls a face.

DAVID
(*to Ken*)
What about the black-haired one?

KEN
She was Turkish. Only been in the country five minutes.

Ken looks at Muriel.

KEN
Whoever marries David, they'll have to tell the Immigration authorities that they're in love with him. There'll be media attention so they'll have to live with him in his flat for at least four months after the marriage. I've worked out the details of the romance which you and Dave will have to stick to. The main thing is to convince people that you two are in love and not doin' this for any cynical motive of mutual gain.

DAVID
What about the red-head?

KEN
You didn't like her.

DAVID
I'm not so sure now.

KEN
I think Mariel might be just what we're lookin' for.

Muriel smiles. She lights a cigarette.

KEN
It's up to you, love. Would you find it difficult to lie?

MURIEL
I could try.

She puffs some smoke towards David.

KEN
Don't rush into a decision, but if you could let us know by tomorrow morning.

SC. 65   INT. FLAT – NIGHT

Muriel enters the dark flat and walks to her bedroom. She stops beside the half-open door of Rhonda's room.

We see Rhonda, asleep, curled up in her bed. Her upper body is supported by pillows. The wheelchair, gleaming silver in the moonlight, stands beside the bed.

Muriel enters her bedroom and closes the door. She moves to the window and inserts a cassette into a tape recorder that sits on the sill. As she looks out at the city lights, Abba's 'Dancing Queen' begins to play.

SC. 66   TITLE CARD

A title card reads: MARIEL'S WEDDING

SC. 67   EXT. CHURCH – DAY

Guests file into an old church in the city. A number of journalists and photographers stand on the stairs, a TV news team sets up near the doors.

SC. 68   INT. CHURCH – DAY

Inside sprigs of jasmine and apple blossom have been attached to the side of each pew by pink satin bows. Floral arrangements adorn the walls and the altar. An elderly organist plays 'Ave Maria'.

Most of the guests are taking seats on the bride's side of the church. On the groom's side sit half a dozen teenage boys and girls, all members of Ken's swimming squad.

Rhonda, dressed conservatively, is wheeled into the church by Berris. Berris wears a floral dress with a matching hat.

> **BERRIS**
> I know you couldn't get up on to the altar, but at least she could have asked you to be a bridesmaid.

> **RHONDA**
> She did.

BERRIS

Why didn't you say yes? You could have been on TV.

RHONDA

I don't want to sit here. I want to sit in the corner.

BERRIS

But no one'll see you over there.

Rhonda attempts to turn her wheelchair. Berris pushes her towards the confessional booths.

BERRIS

If this is your attitude, I don't know why you bothered coming.
(*parks the chair*)
Well, you won't be in anyone's way.

Berris walks off to find a seat. Three giggling bridesmaids enter the church. They see Rhonda and stare. As they approach, Rhonda recognises them as Tania, Janine and Cheryl.

CHERYL
(*shocked*)

Rhonda? Is that you?

RHONDA
(*stunned*)

You're the bridesmaids?

CHERYL

Isn't it fantastic? We always knew Mariel would come good.

JANINE

She's in all the papers.

TANIA
(*cool*)

What happened to you?

RHONDA

I had cancer.

Cheryl and Janine recoil in horror.

RHONDA

It's alright, they cut it out. I won't walk again though.

CHERYL

You were so full of life.

RHONDA

I'm not dead, Cheryl.

JANINE

We better get ready. Mariel's coming.
(*to Rhonda*)
You must be so happy for her.

Cheryl and Janine move back to the entrance of the church. Tania stays behind.

TANIA

I'm divorcing Chook. I suppose I have you to thank for that. I hope I can do the same for you one day.

Tania walks off.

Deidre Chambers sits in a pew behind Bill's lawyers. She slips off her gloves and checks her make-up in a compact.

Brice Nobes, looking dishevelled and depressed, enters the church and sits up the back.

David and Ken (the best man), both wearing suits, sit in a pew before the altar.

DAVID

You told me it'd be a quick civil ceremony.

KEN

It's good she wanted a church wedding – it looks romantic, like you mean it.
(*looks back, frowns*)
All the guests are on her side. I should have hired you some friends.

SC. 69   EXT. CHURCH – DAY

Outside the church, Bill is surrounded by the press.

BILL

I'm not surprised by the charges – the bastards were out to get me from the beginnin'. I jus' wanna say that . . .

But the press are rushing from Bill towards a white Rolls Royce that has pulled up before the church. The driver opens a door to reveal Muriel dressed as a bride. Her gown is the ultimate in bridal excess, made from duchess satin with beaded French chantilly; her tulle veil is as voluminous and white as a small cloud and her train is three metres long.

Muriel is surrounded by press. There is a cacophony of questions, including 'Are you doing it for love or money?' and 'How much are they paying you?' Bill takes Muriel's arm and they walk up the stairs.

BILL

Your mum's comin' to Sydney by bus 'cause I couldn't afford a plane ticket. That's what ya done to me.

MURIEL

Where is she now?

BILL

I don't know. Tryin' to get a taxi, I s'pose. Are you makin' dough on this?

SC. 70   INT. CHURCH – DAY

Tania, Janine and Cheryl stare in awe as Muriel enters the church.

TANIA

Mariel! You're beautiful.

Muriel smiles with satisfaction. She lowers her veil.

The priest steps out on to the altar and beckons to David.

David takes a deep breath and stands with Ken before the priest.

The organist stops playing. The congregation fall silent and stand.

Rhonda looks towards the front entrance of the church.

The church is suddenly filled by the sound of saxophones blaring the opening bars of Abba's 'I Do, I Do, I Do'. The music assails the guests from four different speakers in each corner of the church.

As Anna and Frida sing the opening verse, Muriel appears at the end of the aisle and begins her slow walk to the altar.

The guests stare open-mouthed, stunned.

Rhonda snorts with laughter.

Suppressing a proud grin, Muriel walks down the aisle.

The guests continue to stare in amazement, mouth after mouth wide open.

Tania, Janine and Cheryl, walking behind Muriel, look highly embarrassed.

Bill, escorting Muriel, stares ahead. Every now and then he nods at a passing stunned friend.

Muriel can't help herself and pulls a quick face.

David, a look of indescribable horror on his face, watches his approaching bride. He looks towards the altar.

DAVID

Oh Christ . . . Oh God . . .

KEN

Don't panic. Think of the Games.

Muriel reaches David. Bill steps back.

BILL
(*nodding to David*)

She's all yours, mate.

David looks at Muriel. She pulls a face.

Rhonda watches from her corner.

PRIEST

Father, when you created mankind you willed that man and wife should be one. Bind David and Muriel . . .

MURIEL

Mariel.

PRIEST

. . . Mariel in the loving union of marriage, so that they may be living witness to your divine love in the world.

Deidre Chambers dabs at her eyes with a lace handkerchief.

Berris is crying too. Behind her Brice looks distraught.

Rhonda watches impassively.

PRIEST

David, do you take Mariel to be your wife? Do you promise to be true to her in good times and in bad, and in sickness and in health, to love and honour her all the days of your life.

David looks stunned. Ken elbows him in the side.

DAVID
(*quickly*)

Okay, alright, why not, I do.

PRIEST

Mariel, do you take David to be your husband? Do you
promise to be true to him in good times and in bad, in sickness
and in health, to love and honour him all the days of your life?

MURIEL

I do.

Rhonda looks down.

PRIEST

You have declared your consent before the church. May the
Lord strengthen your consent and fill you with his blessings.
What God has joined, men must not divide.

Rhonda turns her chair and quickly wheels out of the church.

SC. 71   EXT. CHURCH – DAY

*As Rhonda comes out of the door, a taxi pulls up in the street. Betty,
wearing a crumpled mauve dress, struggles to lift her bulk out of the back
seat.*

SC. 72   INT. CHURCH – DAY

David places the ring on Muriel's finger.

DAVID
(*nervous*)

Muriel – Mariel, take this ring as a sign of my . . .

PRIEST
(*prompting*)

Love and fidelity . . .

DAVID
(*struggles to get the words out*)
. . . love and fidelity.
(*quickly*)
In the name of the Father, Son and Holy Spirit.

MURIEL
(*word-perfect*)
David, I take this ring as a sign of your love and fidelity. In the name of the Father, and of the Son, and of the Holy Spirit.

Tania, Janine and Cheryl all have identical tears running down their right cheeks.

PRIEST
I now pronounce you man and wife. Congratulations.
(*to David*)
You can kiss your bride.

David lifts Muriel's veil and gives her a quick peck on the cheek. A couple of press photographers manage to capture the moment on film. The happy congregation burst into applause.

Betty enters and mutters 'Oh' upon seeing the advanced state of the ceremony. She takes a seat up at the back.

David and Muriel sign the register book which lies open on the altar table. The organist plays 'Chorus from Solomon' by Handel.

Ken breathes a sigh of relief.

Tania, Janine and Cheryl move in to congratulate Muriel and David. Deidre moves up to Bill's side and gives him a kiss of congratulations. David shakes hands with Bill.

DAVID
Mr Heslop . . .

BILL
Bill.

DAVID
(*looks at Deidre*)

Mrs Heslop . . .

He kisses Deidre on the cheek. Deidre makes to correct him, but is so moved by the gesture she merely gasps and kisses him back. She grabs Bill's hand.

Betty watches from the back row.

Hand in hand, Muriel and David move up the aisle. Muriel grins at her guests and passes Betty without seeing her.

SC. 73   EXT. CHURCH – DAY

Outside the guests surround the bridal party on the stairs.

MAN
(*shaking David's hand*)

How do you feel?

*Amendment (28/10/93)

KEN
(over-excited)

He's fighting fit.

(grabs David's hand)

★The next gold on this hand will be the gold medal for the 1500 metres.

Tania, Janine and Cheryl chat to a journalist.

TANIA

Mariel and us have been friends for years. We went to Hibiscus Island together.

Muriel, accepting congratulations, looks past the crowd.

A few feet away, the front of Rhonda's wheelchair pokes out from behind the side of the church. Muriel walks towards her.

RHONDA
(as Muriel appears)

I was trying to hide from you.

MURIEL
I saw your wheels. I didn't think you'd come.

RHONDA
I had to see it for myself. Just the bridesmaids were worth it.

MURIEL
I didn't call them, *they* came crawling back to me. The way they picked on me in Porpoise Spit, saying I wouldn't amount to anything, and here I am famous and they're at my wedding. I showed them.

RHONDA
Showed them what?

MURIEL
I'm as good as they are.

RHONDA
(*moves off*)
I have to go. Good luck with whatsisname.

MURIEL
Where you going?

RHONDA
Where do you think? Back to Porpoise Spit with Mum – we're catching a bus out tonight.

MURIEL
I don't want you to.

RHONDA
You should have thought of that before you gave up on me. I couldn't pay all the rent without you, I couldn't even do the shopping. I needed help. I needed a friend.

MURIEL
I mean I don't want you to go back by bus. I bought you two plane tickets.

Rhonda stares at Muriel and then wheels past her.

RHONDA

Go to hell.

MURIEL

I already gave them to your Mum.

Rhonda stops and turns.

RHONDA

You're right. You're a new person.
                    (*angrily*)
And you stink. Mariel Van Arckle stinks. And she's not half the
person Muriel Heslop was.

*Rhonda wheels off. She is quickly surrounded by Tania, Janine and
Cheryl.*

TANIA

Rhonda! Your Mum just told us you're moving back to
Porpoise Spit.

CHERYL

It'll be just like old times.

Rhonda looks horrified. Tania takes hold of her wheelchair.

TANIA
(*to Berris*)
Don't worry about Rhonda, Mrs E, we'll push her around.

Muriel watches as the girls wheel Rhonda away.

SC. 74   INT. DAVID'S APARTMENT – NIGHT

*Muriel and David, still dressed as the bride and groom, enter David's
apartment. It has an unlived-in look and has been decorated by
professionals. A picture window offers an impressive view of the harbour.*

MURIEL

Are you rich?

DAVID

My parents own it.

MURIEL

They didn't come to the wedding.

DAVID

No, they paid for it. They're in Johannesburg.
(*gesturing about the apartment*)
Loungeroom. Kitchen.

In the corner of the lounge is a gym area.

DAVID

Gym. You can use everything but the weights.

David leads Muriel down a hall.

DAVID

Bathroom.
(*indicates a room at the end of the hall*)
My room.

He opens a door on to a guest room containing a single bed.

DAVID

Your room.

Muriel's luggage sits on the floor beside the bed.

DAVID

I'm going downstairs for a swim.

He walks towards his bedroom, but stops and turns.

DAVID

It wasn't just the money, was it?

Muriel shakes her head.

DAVID

What kind of person marries someone they don't know?

MURIEL

You did.

DAVID

I want to win. All my life I've wanted to win.

> Me too.

David enters his bedroom and shuts the door. Muriel enters her room. She sits on the bed and removes her veil. Confetti falls on the parquet floor.

Muriel opens one of her bags to find the photograph of herself and Rhonda on the cruise. She places the photo on a dresser and crosses to the bedroom window.

Visible below is a floodlit swimming pool set into the roof of an adjacent wing of the apartment building. David's small figure, wearing swimmers, walks out on to the roof and dives into the pool. He swims back and forth.

SC. 75   INT. PORPOISE SPIT SUPERMARKET – DAY

In a busy Porpoise Spit supermarket, the check-out shelves display copies of a popular women's magazine which features a cover photo of Muriel in her bridal gown. A blurb reads: Mariel Van Arckle tells 'The Happiest Day of My Life'.

Betty pushes a grocery-laden trolley past the magazines. She walks towards two gossiping women and catches the words '. . . Betty Heslop, Bill Heslop's wife . . .' She smiles and nods hello, but the women turn away.

> BETTY
> (*embarrassed*)

> Oh . . .

She passes the women. A look of discomfort crosses her face.

Betty's shoes are too small and cut into her swollen ankles.

Betty stops before a basket filled with discount massage slippers and selects a pair in her size. She slips off her shoes and puts on the slippers. They fit. She takes a few steps. They feel comfortable.

Betty bends to pick up her old shoes but she can't reach them – she'd have to get down on her knees. She looks embarrassed and pushes the shoes aside with her feet. She wheels her trolley out of the aisle.

She passes a woman shopper at an opposite shelf. The woman turns and watches Betty walk off. It is Dianne, the store detective who arrested Muriel at the wedding. She follows Betty.

Betty, lost in a daydream, stands at a check-out while the check-out girl rings up her groceries. Standing two shoppers behind Betty is Dianne. She looks down.

On Betty's feet are the massage slippers.

The girl rings up the total. Betty snaps out of her reverie and takes money from her purse. The girl counts out Betty's change and Betty steps away from the check-out.

Dianne moves in for the kill.

DIANNE

Excuse me!

Dianne's voice is just loud enough to attract everyone's attention.

DIANNE

I saw you put those slippers on your feet and you haven't paid for them.

BETTY
(looking down at the slippers with genuine surprise)

Oh! I forgot! I meant to pay . . . Oh . . .
(opens her purse)
I'll pay for them now.

DIANNE
(intractable)

Would you accompany me to the office please.

BETTY

Oh. But I have the money . . . I meant to pay . . .

DIANNE
(breaking in)

Just accompany me to the office.

BETTY

I go into daydreams . . .

DIANNE

Do you want me to call a security guard?

Betty looks terrified. Dianne takes Betty by the arm and leads her back into the supermarket. Everybody stares.

DIANNE
(as they walk)

What did you think? That you could steal because you're Bill Heslop's wife? He doesn't run this town any more, he's a joke. He doesn't even live at home. Five counts of taking bribes against him and he still won't resign from the council. The arrogance of it. He might resign after this.

SC. 76   EXT. SUPERMARKET – DAY

Two policemen escort Betty from the supermarket and seat her in a police car. She looks degraded, humiliated.

SC. 77   INT. POLICE STATION – DAY

Late in the afternoon. Betty sits alone in the Sergeant's office. Behind her, in a room across the hall, Bill talks with two policemen. Their voices are barely audible, but we overhear:

BILL

You can see she's not right in the head.

SERGEANT

I'll see what I can do, Bill.

BILL

You're a mate. I won't forget it.

SC. 78   INT. BILL'S CAR – DAY

Bill drives Betty home.

I meant to pay.

Bill stares ahead.

BETTY

I need some help . . . around the house . . . I . . .

Bill switches on the radio and turns up the volume.

SC. 79   INT. HESLOP HOUSE – DAY

Bill is placing the last of his belongings in an old suitcase. Betty stands in the bedroom doorway. Bill closes the suitcase and looks at Betty.

BILL

I'm not comin' back. I want a divorce. I'm marryin' Deidre.

He moves past Betty into the hallway.

BILL
(pause)

You know what they say? They say I wasn't elected to Federal Parliament that time 'cause my family wasn't up to scratch. That's what they say.

Through opened bedroom doors we can see unmade beds, unwashed clothes on the floor, cats sleeping in sunlight.

BILL
(in disgust)

Look at this place. I never 'ad a bloody chance.

Bill walks down the hallway. Betty follows him as far as the lounge. Perry sits slumped in a chair watching television. Bill walks down the stairs.

Betty moves to the verandah doors and watches Bill climb into his car. He drives off.

Betty walks to the centre of the loungeroom. She looks at Perry. In a sudden rage she picks up a magazine and begins to slap him about the head with it.

111

BETTY

Get out! Get out and find a job!

Perry, warding off blows, leaps to his feet.

BETTY

Go on, you layabout! Stop embarrassing your father! You're an
embarrassment!

Perry snatches the magazine from her hands and hurls it across the room.

PERRY
(*shouts*)

You're the embarrassment! Ya mad bitch!

*Perry runs from the house. Betty, breathless from her outburst, stands
alone in the loungeroom. She walks into the kitchen and stops.*

BETTY

Oh . . . Oh . . .

SC. 80   INT. DAVID'S APARTMENT – NIGHT

Muriel, David and Ken sit around the dining-room table.

KEN
(*to Muriel*)

Woman's Day want to do a follow-up to the 'Happiest Day of My
Life' story – 'My First Month of Wedded Bliss' – and *Vogue* want
to do a photo shoot: you in your wedding dress standing on a
diving board.

DAVID

I'm not a diver.

KEN

You're not in the photo.

Muriel smiles. The oven bell rings and she walks to the kitchen.

KEN
(*to Muriel*)

There's a story on you in the *Sun*. I haven't read it yet, but I hear
it's good, very positive about the marriage.

*Muriel takes a hot pizza from the oven and places it on a tray. She
collects some plates.*

DAVID

I could be in the background . . . in the pool.

KEN

They only want Mariel.

Muriel places the pizza on the table.

DAVID
(*looking at the pizza*)

What's this? This isn't food. Where are the vegetables?

MURIEL
(*points out details on the topping*)

There's mushroom and capsicum . . .

DAVID

I don't eat junk.

He stands.

DAVID
(*angrily, to Ken*)

You didn't even ask if she could cook!

MURIEL

I can't cook! I can't type either!

DAVID
(*shouts at Ken*)

I want to be in that photograph! She's my wife! She wouldn't even
be famous if I hadn't married her!

David walks out of the room. A door slams.

KEN

He'll be right once he makes the trials.

Ken cuts himself a slice of pizza.

KEN

This looks great.

SC. 81   EXT. POOL – NIGHT

David does laps in the roof-top pool.

SC. 82   INT. DAVID'S APARTMENT – NIGHT

Muriel sits alone in the loungeroom watching her wedding video. She is step-framing the moment where David places the ring on her finger. The phone beside her chair rings.

MURIEL
(*answering phone*)
Mariel Van Arckle speaking.

There is the sound of a voice sobbing.

MURIEL

Hello . . . ?

JOAN'S VOICE

Muriel . . .

MURIEL

Mariel.

JOAN'S VOICE

Mum's died.

MURIEL

What?

JOAN'S VOICE
We're all at the hospital . . . You have to come home.

Joan begins sobbing again. Muriel looks at the television.

On the television screen the video-player is slowly step-framing an image of a group of people outside the church. We catch Betty, small in the background, smiling at the camera. Then she is gone.

SC. 83   EXT. PORPOISE SPIT – DAY

We are above the clouds. They part to reveal the town of Porpoise Spit. The sound of plane wheels locking into place for landing.

SC. 84   INT. TAXI IN PORPOISE SPIT – DAY

Muriel sits in a taxi as it travels through town.

SC. 85   EXT. HESLOP HOUSE – DAY

The taxi pulls into the drive of the Heslop house. Cicadas buzz. Muriel climbs out of the car.

SC. 86   INT. HESLOP LOUNGEROOM – DAY

She walks up the stairs into the loungeroom. The television is off. Perry sits in a chair, Malcolm loiters in a corner, Penelope talks on the telephone. Deidre Chambers, wearing an apron and rubber gloves, is on her knees scrubbing out a kitchen cupboard. The kitchen, like the loungeroom, looks neat and clean.

> PENELOPE
> (*on phone*)
> The funeral's tomorrow. You coming? Russell's gonna be there. Yeah, I invited him. He says he's gonna bring Alan.

> MURIEL

Hi.

> PERRY
> (*looks up*)

Hi.

Deidre pulls her head out of the cupboard.

Mariel? Is that you?

Deidre, removing her gloves and apron, enters the loungeroom and hugs Muriel. Muriel stiffens.

DEIDRE

Sad loss. She was a dear thing. Isn't David with you?

MURIEL

He couldn't come. He has to train.

DEIDRE

Your Dad's on the other phone. They've being ringing all morning.

Muriel sits on the couch. Deidre sits beside her.

DEIDRE

It was a heart attack. Joanie found her. She was lying on her bed looking peaceful. She didn't suffer. Joanie's a bit upset. She won't come out of her room.

Penelope hangs up the phone and skips out of the back door.

PENELOPE
(*excited*)

All my friends are sending me a card.

DEIDRE

She made the ultimate sacrifice for your father. The Judge will be lenient on him now. He's got the kids to support. She'd be glad in the end her life amounted to something.

A woman who looks exactly like Deidre emerges from the bathroom carrying a bucket of cleaning items.

WOMAN

Deidre, I've finished up in the bathroom. You were right about those cupboards.

DEIDRE
(*stands*)

Let's start on the laundry – it's a big job.

Deidre and the woman leave the lounge.

> PERRY
> (*to Muriel*)

Have you cried yet?

> MURIEL

No.

> PERRY

Me either.

Muriel stands and looks towards the back window. Her eyes widen in shock.

> MURIEL

What happened to the back yard.

Through the window we can see that the grass in the back yard has been scorched black.

> MALCOLM

Mum burnt it.

Muriel opens the back door. The entire yard has been burnt up to the fence line. The charred grass is still smoking. Burn marks stain the bricks at the back of the house.

> MURIEL

Why?

> MALCOLM

She got sick of waiting for Perry to mow it.

SC. 87   INT. HESLOP BEDROOM – DAY

Bill sits at his desk talking on the phone. Muriel enters the bedroom.

> BILL

Battlin' through. Coulda been worse, coulda been cancer. Gotta go now, Ray, me daughter Muriel's 'ere from Sydney. Yeah, thanks for ringin'.

Bill hangs up the phone and stands. He moves to Muriel and they awkwardly hug. Muriel feels odd in his embrace. He breaks the hug and looks at the bed.

> BILL
>
> Found 'er on the bed. We got 'er to the 'ospital, but there was nothin' they could do. I knew it was over when they gave me 'er watch.

Bill looks at Muriel.

> BILL
>
> We 'ave to stick together now, okay? For ever.

The phone rings.

> BILL
> (*answering phone*)
>
> Bill Heslop. Jack McGrath, 'ow are ya? Yeah. Yeah. Could 'ave been worse, coulda been cancer.
> (*sits*)
> I don' know. I think she's better off out of it.

SC. 88   INT. MURIEL'S OLD BEDROOM – DAY

Joan sits on her bed, a photo album on her lap. There is a small knock on the door and Muriel enters the room.

> MURIEL
>
> Hi.

She sits in a chair beside the bed.

> JOAN
>
> What am I gonna do without 'er? She used to do all me readin' for me, all me forms. I was so worried about 'er. She used to sleep so quiet. I'd say 'Mum, are you okay?' an' she'd say 'I'm fine, go back to bed.' Sometimes I'd think people were followin' me, but Mum said they weren't. I don' know . . . maybe they are.

> MURIEL
>
> They're not following you, Joanie.

Muriel takes the photo album from Joan's lap.

Her photo album.

Muriel opens the album to find a small pile of newspaper clippings. They are all reports on Muriel's wedding.

Muriel looks at the black and white photo of Bill and Betty on their wedding day. They are seated in the back of a car, both smiling into the camera. Betty, in her bridal gown, looks very pretty: thin, bright-eyed, aged about twenty. Bill looks a naïve, skinny, big-eared youth.

She turns the pages. We glimpse photos that show Betty at different stages in her married life. Bill appears less frequently, and Betty's arms fill with children; she becomes fatter and shorter.

The last photo in the album is a colour photo taken about two years ago. It shows Bill, sitting at a large table in a restaurant, surrounded by his mates. Betty sits at the end of the table. She is partially obscured by a large man. She smiles into the camera.

JOAN
(*ruefully looking at the photo*)
Everyone's gonna say it was 'cause she was fat.

MURIEL
It was because she was fat.
(*pause*)
You should lose weight, Joanie.

JOAN
(*quietly*)

She took pills.

MURIEL

For her heart?

JOAN

Sleeping pills.

It takes a moment for the words to sink into Muriel.

JOAN

They was next to 'er when I found 'er, an' after Doctor Farrell come they were gone. I asked what 'appened to 'em, an' Dad said 'e didn't want anyone to know. Doctor Farrell said Dad 'ad been through enough. I don' know, maybe 'e 'as.

(*nods*)

I think they're followin' 'im, too.

SC. 89   INT. CHURCH IN PORPOISE SPIT – DAY

Betty's small coffin stands in the aisle before the altar.

In a front pew Muriel sits with Bill and the family. Perry has shaved. Penelope waves to a nearby friend. Deidre Chambers sits behind them. Mourners are still filing into the church. Bill, surveying the turnout, looks pleased.

Up the back a camera crew is shooting a wideshot of the interior of the church. Near them sit a row of journalists all armed with notebooks and tape-recorders.

BILL

Look at them mongrels. I got a surprise for them.

Later, and the mourners stand singing a hymn. The hymn ends and everyone sits. An elderly Irish priest steps up to the lectern. Bill looks expectant.

OLD PRIEST

I have a telegram to read.

BILL
(*to Perry*)

Keep your eye on them journalist bastards.

Perry turns and looks to the back of the church.

OLD PRIEST
(*reading telegram*)

'To Bill Heslop and family. Hazel and I were sorry to hear of the passing of Betty. We are thinking of you in your time of sorrow.' Signed The Honorable Bob Hawke, former Prime Minister of Australia.

BILL
(*to Perry*)

What are they doin'?

PERRY

Writin' it down.

The journalists are all scribbling furiously into notebooks.

BILL
(*pleased*)

I bet they are. Put that in ya papers, ya mongrel bastards. I still got friends.

(*to Muriel*)

What other family gets a telegram from a former Prime Minister when somebody dies? Hey? I'm not forgotten.

Muriel has observed all this with a look of shocked recognition. She becomes aware of the old priest's eulogy.

OLD PRIEST

Betty Heslop lived for her family and found fulfilment in their achievements. She was very happy about her daughter Mariel's marriage and attending the wedding in Sydney was one of the highlights of her life.

Muriel sits quietly for a moment. The eulogy continues, but she does not hear it. She looks at her mother's coffin, then stands and walks up the aisle.

SC. 90   EXT. CHURCH – DAY

Muriel walks out of the church into the sunshine. She gasps and her breath comes fast.

DAVID'S VOICE

Mariel.

She looks up to see David standing beside a rental car parked before the church. Muriel stares at him as he slowly approaches. He stops before her.

DAVID
(*with a small shrug*)

I thought I should be with you.

Muriel rests her head on his shoulder and begins to sob. He tentatively puts his arms around her. She hugs him close.

SC. 91   INT. HOTEL ROOM IN PORPOISE SPIT – DAY

In a small hotel room in town, Muriel sits on the end of David's bed. He emerges from the bathroom with a glass of water. Muriel takes it and David sits beside her.

MURIEL

I thought I was so different. A new person. But I'm not. I'm the same as him.

Muriel looks close to tears again. David takes the glass from her and places it on the floor. He looks at her and moves some hair away from her face.

Muriel looks up at him. David leans in and gently kisses her.

Muriel responds, needing the contact.

They slowly lie back on the bed.

SC. 92   INT. HOTEL ROOM IN PORPOISE SPIT – DAY

The next day, Muriel and David lie naked in the dim light of early morning. Muriel is awake. She looks at David, who is sleeping, and then quietly slips out of his arms.

She quickly dresses and then dials the telephone. She orders a taxi in a soft voice, but David awakens. Muriel sits on the side of the bed.

MURIEL

I can't stay married to you, David. I have to stop lying now. I
tell so many lies . . . one day I won't know I'm doing it.
(*pause*)
I don't love you.

DAVID

I don't love you either, but . . . I don't know, I think I could
like having you around.

Muriel shakes her head.

DAVID
(*pause*)
You can't annul us, we consummated it three times.

Muriel smiles.

MURIEL
I'll give you the money back.

DAVID

It's yours.

Muriel places her wedding ring on the bedside table. She walks to the door, opens it and turns.

MURIEL

Good luck in the Games.

DAVID

You too.

She leaves the room. David lies back and looks at the roof.

SC. 93   EXT. HESLOP HOUSE – DAY

A taxi pulls up before the Heslop house. A truck, bearing the logo 'Roll-a-Lawn', is parked in the drive. Muriel climbs out of the taxi and looks towards the house.

Bill and a man in overalls stand in the blackened back yard. Muriel walks towards them.

LAWN MAN
(using a pocket calculator)
$100 for the rotary hoe . . . 130 metres of topsoil at $30.00 a metre
. . . instant lawn $3.75 a roll, $1.25 per metre for laying . . . comes
to . . . $4,675.00

Bill, stunned, gives a small nod. Muriel stops nearby.

BILL

How ya house extensions goin'? I had trouble gettin' council
approval for that second storey, I'll tell ya.

The man smiles, nods.

BILL

The council get on to ya 'bout that footy field? I told 'em you
give that job to Ross McLennan.

LAWN MAN
(nods)

They did. Thanks, Bill.

BILL

No worries. How much was it again?

LAWN MAN

$4,675.00

BILL

(*after an awkward pause*)

Can't help me out with a discount, can ya?

LAWN MAN

Sorry, Bill. Business isn't good. You know how it is.

(*after a beat*)

Call me when you know what you're gonna do.

He walks back to his truck. Bill looks at Muriel.

BILL

Why'd she burn the back yard. I don' understand it.

(*pause*)

We gotta stick together. You gotta 'elp me with the kids.

MURIEL

What about Deidre?

BILL

She'll lend a hand. But I don't think she's too keen on marryin' me now that livin' with the kids has come into the picture. Someone 'as to look after 'em.

MURIEL

It has to be you, Dad.

BILL

You owe me, Muriel.

MURIEL

I owe you money.

She gives him a cheque.

MURIEL

It's not all of it – I'll pay the rest off when I get back to Sydney and get a job.

BILL

So you're not gonna 'elp me out, is that it?

MURIEL

You owe us, Dad. We're not useless. We never were. You're looking after the kids. And you're gonna tell them they're not useless.

Bill is silent for a moment.

BILL

'Ow 'bout that telegram from Bob Hawke.

MURIEL

How'd you get that?

BILL

I phoned his office. I was almost a Member of 'is Government. Remember 'ow close it was? Fourteen votes I needed. Nobody knew who'd won for three days until the postal votes come in . . . for three days I was almost there.

(*pause*)

I couldn't win a chook raffle now. I've resigned from Council. I'm unemployed. I gotta go on the dole. Imagine the look on their faces when I walk into that dole office.

(*pause*)

I know what I done.

Bill looks around the yard, his face turned away.

BILL

Ya reap what ya sow, don' ya? You'd think I'd 'ave learnt that growin' up on a farm. Ya reap what ya sow.

The back door of the house opens and Joan steps on to the landing.

JOAN

Dad, the cricket's started.

Bill does not respond.

MURIEL

Hi, Joan.

126

BILL
(*gathering himself together, to Joan*)
Muriel's goin' back to Sydney.

JOAN
Are ya? I thought you was stayin' with us.

BILL
(*to Muriel*)
Keep in touch.

MURIEL
'Bye, Dad.

Muriel leaves the yard.

JOAN
You wan' me to open ya a can of beer?

BILL
That'd be lovely, Joanie. I'll be with ya in a sec.

Joan smiles and enters the house. Bill stands alone in the yard.

SC. 94   INT. BERRIS'S HOUSE – DAY

Rhonda sits in her wheelchair in her mother's tidy loungeroom. She is surrounded by Tania, Janine and Cheryl. Berris emerges from the kitchen with tea and cakes.

TANIA
I'm giving it another chance with Chook – as soon as he gets out of the correction centre. They've accused him of raping a Japanese tourist, which is ridiculous – Chook hates the Japanese.

CHERYL
We better fly. We're meeting Rose Biggs for lunch.

RHONDA
(*surprised*)
Rose Biggs? You're friends with her?

TANIA
(*with a shrug*)
Once we got to know her, we found out she was just like us.

RHONDA
But . . . Rose Biggs sucked your husband's cock.

BERRIS
(*shocked*)
Rhonda!

RHONDA
Well she did!

TANIA
I know, but . . . well . . .
(*blurts it out*)
I sucked her husband's cock and it made me realise we all make mistakes.

MURIEL'S VOICE
Hi.

Everyone turns and looks to the entrance of the lounge.

Where Muriel stands. Behind her we can see the open front door.

TANIA
Mariel!

BERRIS
Mariel!

MURIEL
Muriel.

BERRIS
(*stands*)
What a surprise. Rhonda, Mariel – Muriel's come to visit you.

Rhonda glares at Muriel.

MURIEL
Actually, I've come to take Rhonda back to Sydney.

BERRIS
You what?

MURIEL
I want to take Rhonda back to Sydney. I've got a taxi outside and two plane tickets.

TANIA
What about your husband?

MURIEL
We broke up.

TANIA
(*quietly to Janine*)
I knew it wouldn't last.

RHONDA
(*to Muriel*)
What makes you think I'd go anywhere with you?

MURIEL
Because I'm your friend.

BERRIS
(*furious*)
Muriel, you can't come barging in here without warning trying to turn Rhonda against the people who love her
(*pointedly*)
– against the people who were there when she needed them.

RHONDA
Yes, she can.

Berris, horrified, looks at Rhonda.

RHONDA
Sorry, Mum. You know I love you, but you drive me crazy.
(*looks at Tania, Janine and Cheryl*)
And you three . . . what a bunch of cocksuckers.

The girls gasp. Muriel takes the wheelchair and begins to push Rhonda from the room. Tania stands.

TANIA

Muriel!

Muriel turns.

TANIA

You always were nothing but a fat ugly pointless pig.

Muriel stares at Tania for a moment.

MURIEL
(*simply and without malice*)

Liar.

TANIA
(*offended*)

You can't call me that!

But Muriel is already pushing Rhonda out of the house.

SC. 95   EXT. BERRIS'S HOUSE – DAY

Muriel pushes Rhonda down the driveway to a waiting taxi. Berris, Tania, Janine and Cheryl follow.

TANIA
(*outraged*)

Who do you think you are to call me that?! I'm married! I'm beautiful!

Muriel and Rhonda shriek with laughter. Rhonda slides on to the back seat. The driver stows the wheelchair in the boot.

RHONDA

See you, Mum!

Berris looks miserable, but braves a farewell smile.

Muriel sits beside Rhonda. The taxi drives off.

SC. 96   INT. TAXI – DAY

Rhonda looks out her window.

RHONDA

'Bye street!

They pass the Porpoise Spit Mall.

RHONDA

G'Bye Mall!

MURIEL
(*looking out her window*)

'Bye Waterworld!

RHONDA

'Bye Plaza!

The taxi races through town.

MURIEL

Goodbye beach!

RHONDA

'Bye highrises!

MURIEL AND RHONDA
(*shouting*)

Goodbye Porpoise Spit!

Muriel looks out her window. A rueful look crosses her face, but it is soon replaced by a smile.

SC. 97   EXT. PORPOISE SPIT ROAD — DAY

The taxi roars past a sign which reads: You Are Leaving Porpoise Spit. A cartoon porpoise says in a word balloon: Missing You Already!

131

CIBY 2000
presents in association with
Australian Film Finance Corporation
A House and Moorhouse Films Production
A film by P.J. Hogan
MURIEL'S WEDDING

Cast:

TONI COLLETTE	Muriel
BILL HUNTER	Bill
RACHEL GRIFFITHS	Rhonda
JEANIE DRYNAN	Betty
GENNIE NEVINSON	Deidre
MATT DAY	Brice
DANIEL LAPAINE	David Van Arckle
SOPHIE LEE	Tania
BELINDA JARRETT	Janine
ROSALIND HAMMOND	Cheryl
PIPPA GRANDISON	Nicole
CHRIS HAYWOOD	Ken Blundell
DANIEL WYLLIE	Perry
GABBY MILLGATE	Joan
KATIE SAUNDERS	Penelope
DENE KERMOND	Malcolm
SUSAN PRIOR	Girl at Wedding
NATHAN KAYE	Chook
CECILY POLSON	Tania's Mother
ROB STEELE	Higgins
GENEVIEVE PICOT	Store Detective
RICHARD SUTHERLAND	Constable Saunders
STEVE SMITH	Constable Gillespie
JEAMIN LEE	Chinese Waitress
JON-CLAIRE LEE	Chinese Maître D'
KUNI HASHIMOTO	Akira
KEN SENGA	Victor Keinosuke
DES RODGERS	Island M.C.

ROHAN JONES	Restaurant Boys
SCOTT HALL-WATSON	
CRAIG OLSON	
JUSTIN WITHAM	
RODNEY ARNOLD	Ejected Diner
BARRY CROCKER	Himself
STEVE COX	Cruise Taxi Driver
KEVIN COPELAND	Sailors
JAMES SCHRAMKO	
RICHARD MORECROFT	Himself
RICHARD CARTER	Federal Policeman
JOHN GADEN	Doctor
HEATHER MITCHELL	Bridal Manageress #1
HEIDI LAPAINE	Bridal Assistant #1
DIANE SMITH	Physiotherapist
DARRIN KLIMEK	Rhonda's Taxi Driver
PENNE HACKFORTH-JONES	Bridal Manageress #2
KIRSTY HINCHCLIFFE	Bridal Assistant #2
ROBERT ALEXANDER	Barrister
TROY HARDY	Young Boy
ROBYN PITT OWEN	Singer at Muriel's Wedding
ANNIE BYRON	Rhonda's Mother
JACQUELINE LINKE	Press at Muriel's Wedding
ALVARO MARQUES	
FIONA SULLIVAN	
INEKE RAPP	
JULIAN GARNER	
VINCENT BALL	Priest
JOHN HOARE	Well-wisher at Muriel's Wedding
FRANKIE DAVIDSON	Sergeant
LOUISE CULLEN	Deidre's Friend
BASIL CLARKE	Funeral Priest
JOHN WALTON	Taxi Driver

Crew:

Written and directed by	P. J. HOGAN
Produced by	LYNDA HOUSE &
	JOCELYN MOORHOUSE
Associate Producers	MICHAEL D. AGLION &
	TONY MAHOOD
Casting	ALISON BARRETT
Film Editor	JILL BILCOCK
Director of Photography	MARTIN McGRATH A.C.S.
Production Designer	PATRICK REARDON
Costume Designer	TERRY RYAN
Sound	DAVID LEE
	GLENN NEWNHAM
	LIVIA RUZIC
	ROGER SAVAGE
Original Music	PETER BEST
Production Co-ordinator	ROWENA TALACKO
Production Secretary	SHARON GERUSSI
Production Accountant	JILL STEELE
	MONEYPENNY SERVICES
Assistant Accountant	SANDIE MORRIS
Post Production Accountant	MANDY CARTER
Production Runner	MARTIN WILLIAMS
Location Manager	PATRICIA BLUNT
1st Assistant Director	TONY MAHOOD
2nd Assistant Director	JOHN MARTIN
3rd Assistant Director	KAREN MAHOOD
Script Supervisor	DAPHNE PARIS
Camera Operator	DAVID WILLIAMSON
Focus Puller	DARRIN KEOUGH
Clapper Loader	BRETT MATTHEWS
Camera Attachments	SALLY GRAY
	JOHN FORREST
Key Grip	BRETT McDOWELL
Grip	JOHN TATE
Gaffer	DAVID PARKINSON

Best Boys	PETER MALONEY
	GREG RAWSON
Electrics	ANDREW MOORE
	DARRYN FOX
Boom Operator	JACK FRIEDMAN
Art Director	HUGH BATEUP
Art Department Co-ordinator	CHRISTINA NORMAN
Set Decorators	JANE MURPHY
	GLEN W. JOHNSON
Stand-by Props	JAMES COX
Art Department Assistants	DIANNE BENNETT
	PHILIPA PLAYFORD
Art Department Runner	PETER FORBES
SFX Co-ordinator	RAY FOWLER
Hair & Make-up Supervisor	NORIKO WATANABE
Hairdresser	JAN 'ZIGGY' ZEIGENBEIN
Hair & Make-up Assistant	NOREEN WILKIE
David's Body by	MADISON
Wardrobe Supervisor	MICHELE LEONARD
Stand-by Wardrobe	HEATHER LAURIE
Costume Construction	SUSANNE 'MOUSE' HEAD
Wardrobe Assistant	MANDY SEDAWIE
Assistants to Alison Barrett	KRISTIN WHITFIELD
	TRICIA McASKILL
Extras Casting	GABRIELLE HEALY
Extras Casting Assistant	SANDRA OOSTERMAN
Stunt Co-ordinator	ROCKY McDONALD
Dialogue Coach	VICTORIA MIELEWSKA
Choreographer	JOHN O'CONNELL
Stills Photographer	ROBERT McFARLANE
Caterers	EAT AND SHOOT THROUGH
	ROBERT JANG
Unit Manager	SIMON HAWKINS
Unit Assistants	PHILLIP TAYLOR
	PAUL NAYLOR
	SHANE NAYLOR
Assembly Editor	JANE MORAN
Assistant Editor	CLEO MYLES

Editing Attachment	JEREMY LINES
Foley	GERARD LONG
	STEVE BURGESS
ADR Recordist	PAUL PIROLA
Assistant Sound Editor	JAMES HARVEY
Sound Mixed at	SOUNDFIRM, Melbourne
Soundfirm Liaison	HELEN FIELD
Dolby Stereo Consultant	STEVE MURPHY
Marketing Consultant	FRAN LANIGAN
Travel	TRAVEL TOO – GREG HELMERS
Couriers	WIZ COURIERS (Melbourne)
	BOND COURIERS (Sydney)
Camera Equipment	LEMAC FILM & VIDEO EQUIPMENT
Laboratory: Shoot	ATLAB
Laboratory Liaison	IAN RUSSELL
Opticals	ROGER COWLAND
Laboratory: Post Production	CINEVEX
Laboratory Liaison	IAN ANDERSON
Negative Matching	ROHAN WILSON
Grader	IAN LETCHER
Film Stock	EASTMAN KODAK
Title Design	PETER LONG
Titles	OPTICAL & GRAPHIC
Release Script	JO STEWART
Australasian Distributors	ROADSHOW FILM DISTRIBUTORS
Completion Guarantor	FILM FINANCES LIMITED
	ANTONIA BARNARD
Insurance	STEEVES LUMLEY
	TONY LEONARD
Legal	ROTH WARREN
	BRYCE MENZIES
Bank	ST. GEORGE PARTNERSHIP BANKING LIMITED

Additional Crew – Queensland

Production Runner	DAMIEN ROSSI
Location Manager	RUSSELL BOYD
Unit Manager	NICK FENBY
3rd Assistant Director	ANGELA McPHERSON
Video Split Operator	HEATH WILLIAMSON
Gaffer	KEN MOFFAT
Best Boy	MURRAY HEAD
Grip	GARY SHEARSMITH
Caterer	ELEETS FILM CATERING
	DOUG STEELE
Make-up Assistants	CAROLYN NOTT
	MARG ARCHMAN
Electrician	NICK ADAM
Helicopter Pilot	JEFF McTAGGART
Camera Operator (Helicopter)	ANDREW FLANNIGAN
Music Supervisor	CHRIS GOUGH, MANA

Music

"Dancing Queen" "Waterloo" "Fernando" "Mamma Mia" "I do, I do, I do, I do, I do" (Andersson/Ulvaeus/Anderson) Published for the World by Union Songs AB Performed by Abba, courtesy of PolyGram Pty Limited. Dancing Queen bridal arrangement by Peter Best, Vocals Blazey Best

"The Tide is High" (J. Holt), Published by Sparta Florida Music Group Ltd. Performed by Blondie, courtesy of EMI Music Australia.

"Sugar Baby Love" (Waddington/Bickerton), Published by Warner Chappell Music performed by the Rubettes, courtesy of PolyGram Australia

"T Shirt & Jeans" (McLean/Thorp/Dzajovsky) Published by Mana/Warner Music. Performed by Razorbrain, courtesy of EMI Music Australia

"I Go to Rio" (Allen/Anderson), Published by Irving Music Inc. Used with permission of Rondor Music Australia Pty Ltd. Performed by Peter Allen, courtesy of A&M Records Inc/PolyGram Australia

"We've Only Just Begun" (Williams/Nichols) Published by Irving Music Inc/Woolnough Music. Used with permission of Rondor Music Australia Pty Ltd

"Hotcha" "Coffee & Tea" (Peter Best) Published by Best Results Pty Ltd. Performed by A.A. Aardvaark

Original Music recorded and mixed at VAUCLUSE DIGITAL (Sydney) and METROPOLIS (Melbourne)

Recording & Mixing Engineer – DAVID HEMMINGS

Choir
Organist – DAVID PITT OWEN
Congregation – ST MARY'S CHURCH, Waverly

DOLBY STEREO IN SELECTED THEATRES

Good Morning Australia with Bert Newton by courtesy of NETWORK TEN AUSTRALIA, BERT NEWTON & JOHN-MICHAEL HOWSON

Royal Wedding of HRH The Prince of Wales & Lady Diana Spencer BBC ENTERPRISES UK

Wardrobe courtesy of ROGER DAVID MENSWEAR

GUESS WATCHES TAROCASH MENSWEAR STIKMAN CLOTHING SUNUP SWIMWEAR CORAL REEF SWIMWEAR

Special thanks to
PHILIPPA FINNEY, SARAH FINNEY, CHRIS FITCHETT, KIM DALTON, WENDY PALMER, LOUISE WIGNALL, JANE CAMPION, HELENA HOGAN, DOWIE HOGAN, BENNY ANDERSSON, BJORN ULVAEUS, GOREL HANSER

Financed by CIBY 2000 in association with AUSTRALIAN FILM FINANCE CORPORATION LIMITED

DEVELOPED AND PRODUCED WITH THE ASSISTANCE OF FILM VICTORIA

Developed with the assistance of FILM QUEENSLAND and the PACIFIC
FILM & TELEVISION COMMISSION Project developed with the
assistance of the AUSTRALIAN FILM COMMISSION

This film was produced with the assistance of the NEW SOUTH WALES
FILM AND TELEVISION OFFICE, Sydney, Australia.

Story by P.J. HOGAN & JOCELYN MOORHOUSE

Distributed by Buena Vista International (UK) Ltd